Challenges & Blessings

By

H. Anne Sinotte

To Marilyn

Best Wishes

H A Sinotte

Oct. 19, 2013

H. Anne Sinotte

This book is dedicated to:

*Every person who has experienced
or is presently experiencing the effects
of a life-altering accident
OR
To any person dealing with a terminal illness.*

This book is especially dedicated to:

*My husband Randy and sons Kevin & Brad.
Your light shines forever in my heart and soul.*

*All my love always
Anne / Mom*

H. Anne Sinotte

H. Anne Sinotte

Acknowledgements

This project would not have been completed without the support I received from other sources, throughout the process. I extend my heartfelt gratitude to the following people for their role in helping my dream become a reality.

The first person I wish to thank is my psychologist Dr. Alan MacLeod, who in 2007 when treating me for Post Traumatic Stress Disorder and Depression recognized my ability to articulate words on paper. He suggested that I write about my 2006 accident, in hopes of inspiring other accident victims. His encouragement and belief in me helped me to restore a modicum of self-worth and to once again have faith in myself. I thank you so much Dr. MacLeod, for your insight and for extending to me this bold new challenge.

To my husband Randy, for allowing me the time to write, edit, type and format this book. Time, which could often have been used to do other things together.

To my sons, Kevin and Brad for understanding my vision and encouraging me to put it in print.

H. Anne Sinotte

To my brother Mark, I thank you for your time and expertise in assisting me with the formatting of this book. I could not have done this without your help and patience, so I extend to you my utmost gratitude.

To all my family and friends, who permitted me to use their real names in this book. This added authenticity to the accounts in the book. Names of professionals and institutions were not disclosed. Fictitious names were used solely out of respect for privacy and professionalism.

Last but certainly not least, I thank my Lord and Saviour for allowing me the time to see this book to completion.

With the support, encouragement and love of so many people, this was a work of passion that I poured my heart and soul into, and I believe it was one of my finest achievements.

H. Anne Sinotte

CHALLENGES & BLESSINGS

Prologue

In order to appreciate and understand my story, one must first have a grasp of the person I was prior to this life-altering trauma.

This is a true story of courage after adversity, frustration, incredible personal loss and the determination that gave me hope to rebuild my life with physical modifications and first hand insight into the challenges, both physical and emotional, faced every day by the physically disabled. I have experienced both lives, the so-called "normal" life and the physically challenged life.

This surreal experience has not only been heart-wrenching but has enlightened me to share the realities of this trauma with others in hopes of promoting a greater awareness in others minds, to the obstacles encountered by the physically challenged.

H. Anne Sinotte

H. Anne Sinotte

Background

At the time of my accident on February 11, 2006, I was a 54-year-old wife, mother of 2 adult sons and I was employed part-time as a registered nurse in a Long Term Care facility. I have always been extremely independent and single-handedly took charge of all household cleaning, cooking, baking, laundry, grocery shopping, some gardening, arranged all social engagements and shopped for gifts for all occasions.

I have been involved in some volunteer community work throughout the years, including various fund-raising activities for the Cancer Society and The Heart and Stroke Foundation. I have also planned and organized golf tournaments with proceeds directed to specific charities.

My hobbies and past-times are numerous. I enjoy many handcrafts such as knitting, crocheting, sewing and other homemade projects. I derive much pleasure from leisure or speed walking with my husband Randy and he and I also enjoy having a round of golf together. Another great past time for me is designing interior house plans including the present house we now reside in.

I am a two-time breast cancer survivor. In recent years I have participated in the Cancer Relay For Life survivor's lap with great pride for being one of the fortunate examples of hope.

One of my greatest passions is working in Long Term Care, caring and advocating for the frail elderly. This can often times be very frustrating for many reasons but it can also be extremely rewarding to realize that my actions and compassion can truly make a difference in another person's life.

My favourite time of year is without a doubt Christmas. I love to decorate the house from top to bottom, bake cookies and squares, sing Christmas carols, enjoy the beautiful displays in stores and throughout the community and most important of all spending time with family and friends.

My strongest traits are integrity, compassion and generosity. My weakest traits include being too soft hearted and taking matters too seriously and personal to the extent of becoming inappropriately defensive.

H. Anne Sinotte

* * * * *

As you read through this book, you will note that there are chapters with some repetitive facts. This repetition was deliberate in some cases so that the reader did not have to back track to retrieve information, in other areas repetition reinforced material that I thought was important.

H. Anne Sinotte

H. Anne Sinotte

Expect Miracles
By Dr. Wayne Dyers

The phrase I expect miracles is
How you feel when you live each day In-Spirit

You leave the world of
Anxiety, fear, doubt and impossibility and
Enter a new, wonderful world
Where all things are possible

Everything that you need or want in your life
Will begin to arrive In-Spirit:
The right people will show up
The financing will be attracted
To your enthusiasm and commitment AND
You'll be a source of inspiration to others.

H. Anne Sinotte

H. Anne Sinotte

Part One

H. Anne Sinotte

H. Anne Sinotte

*There is much in the world to make us afraid.
There is much more in our faith to make us
unafraid.*
Frederick W. Cropp

Chapter One
The Accident

In February 2006, my husband Randy and I went on a four-day snowmobiling trip to a resort in the Muskoka's. As we hadn't had a vacation in a few years we were really looking forward to this mini getaway with seven other acquaintances. The trails were scenic and exhilarating. In the past I have always been a passenger on a snowmobile but on the third day of our trip the group we were with persuaded me to drive a machine by myself. I was encouraged by everyone in our group, except my husband to drive one of the machines by myself. They all explained that the real joy was in driving as opposed to being a passenger. I declined the offer by stating that I had never driven a snowmobile before and thought it would be more appropriate to first drive a machine in an open area such as the lake, where there were no obstructions. I figured that this was the best way to get a feel for the machine and how to properly and safely drive it. The group explained that there was nothing to it and after several attempts of declining their offer, I relented and agreed to try it. My husband reminded me that I didn't have to drive if I was uncomfortable with the idea. Two of the seasoned drivers then proceeded to give me a "crash" course on driving the machine and familiarized me with the brakes, power etc. They also reassured me that we would travel at slower speeds.

So after receiving the instructions, I donned my helmet, took a deep breath and we were on our way again in single file with me driving third last. At first I was a little frightened but I drove slowly and enjoyed the challenge. The bends and hills on the trail presented with some challenges, but I also found the experience quite exhilarating. After a few minutes of driving, I began to feel more comfortable and competent in the handling of the machine. This enjoyment was short-lived. I guess I was driving for about fifteen to twenty minutes, when I approached a steeper hill. I partially applied the brakes in an attempt to decrease my speed as I descended the slope. I was having difficulty

H. Anne Sinotte

keeping the skis of the machine on the trail. At the bottom of the hill was a patch of ice that sent the machine off the trail. The left side skis were now sitting above the trail, putting the machine on an elevated slant on the left side. I felt frightened now because I was having difficulty controlling the machine. At this time I sensed that I was in danger, but still fought to keep the machine on the trail. I knew that something was dreadfully wrong.................................I saw my life flash before my eyes...........................lurking just ahead was a huge tree...................................

* * * * *

My next recollection was coming too lying flat in the snow. There were people all around me and someone was crouched over me, stabilizing my neck and head. Everyone was talking but I didn't know where I was or what had happened. I remember thinking, "who are all of these people?" My vision was blurred and obscured and I felt the warm blood running down my face in contrast to the cold winter temperatures. I remember feeling excruciating pain in my head, back, right hand and right leg before I once again drifted into an unconscious state.

H. Anne Sinotte

My recollection of the accident and the days to follow were sketchy at best, as I continued to slip in and out of consciousness. Someone activated 911. I do not remember the paramedics attending and assessing me or of being placed on a scoop stretcher at the scene or of being transported by sled to the awaiting ground ambulance. Nor do I remember Randy being by my side in the ambulance while enrooted to the nearest local Hospital.

Once arriving at the hospital, I was again evaluated and underwent a battery of tests...blood work, x-rays, CT scan and cognitive testing. I vaguely remember the doctor speaking to me in a soft, compassionate manner, telling me that I was involved in a snowmobile accident and that I had sustained multiple, severe injuries. Doctors and nurses worked on me for hours, cleaning me up from all the blood loss and suturing the laceration below my right eyebrow, which was one of the areas of impact with the tree. I remember hearing someone comment that my haemoglobin was 63. Hearing that information, caused me to become anxious because as a nurse I know that this haemoglobin value is half the therapeutic level for a female. I remember the nurse trying to remove rings from my fingers and I remember giving her permission to cut the rings off because she told me

H. Anne Sinotte

my circulation was diminished as a result of extreme swelling to my right hand. I remember being told that I was going to x-ray but I do not remember having the x-rays done. At various times, I vaguely remember seeing Randy's panicked and grief-stricken face.

In my lucid moments, I remembered the pain being excruciating. After several hours the emergency room doctor informed me that my injuries were too many and too complex for this hospital and therefore I would be transferred to a major trauma Hospital in Toronto, because it was better equipped physically and with the specialized personnel for my multiple traumas. The doctor also informed me what my injuries consisted of but I can't honestly say that this information registered. All that did penetrate my thoughts was that there was a great deal wrong with me and that what was wrong with me was of a serious nature. Having heard all that, it was no wonder I had to be sent to a Toronto hospital.

My memory of being airlifted by helicopter to the Toronto hospital is almost non-existent. I remember being outdoors on a stretcher, which was taking me to the helicopter. The pavement was very bumpy which exacerbated the pain in my right leg to the extent that the paramedics stopped pushing the stretcher and administered analgesic to me before placing me in the helicopter. The paramedics on board the chopper were extremely attentive and reacted immediately to every groan, sound or movement I made. At times the pain seemed to explode through my body like fireworks on Canada Day.

I became conscious once again when I arrived in the trauma room at the General hospital, as a soft-spoken, compassionate nurse greeted me. She must have seen the fear in my eyes because she immediately tried to console me by telling me I would be well taken care of. As my eyes took in the numerous doctors and hospital personnel attending to me, it was the first time I realized how critical my condition was and I started to question my mortality. The atmosphere was overwhelming as specialists were examining every inch of me simultaneously. As the specialists poked and probed, they fired questions at me and it took all my strength to give the correct answer to the appropriate source. It wasn't long afterwards that I once again slipped into unconsciousness.

The next time I awakened it was late that evening and I was in my own hospital room. When I looked

H. Anne Sinotte

up my husband Randy and younger brother Mark were standing at the end of my bed. I was hooked up to a number of tubes, my right eye had a patch on it and I was receiving oxygen. I felt like a Mack truck hit me as every inch of my body was riddled with pain. I made several attempts to speak to Randy and Mark but my voice was barely audible, my speech was slow, slurred and garbled, my vision was blurred and my concentration was next to nil...I drifted back to sleep. I continued to drift in and out of sleep for the next two weeks.

H. Anne Sinotte

The soul would have no rainbow had the eyes no tears.
John Vance Cheney

<u>Chapter Two</u>
<u>Assessment & Surgery</u>

The next few days are a blur as I was in and out of consciousness, likely due to being heavily sedated. The doctors informed me that once I was stabilized and an operating room could be secured, I would require several surgeries to repair my damaged body. Repeatedly, the doctors informed me of the severity of my injuries and the long road to recovery that lay ahead. I had several doctors attending to me including internists, orthopods and an ophthalmologist. One by one they informed me that my right hand was fractured in four places, my right tibia was shattered along with my knee, my right first rib was fractured which explained the shortness of breath I experienced and my cognitive state was compromised as a result of the head injury and temporary loss of consciousness. When the ophthalmologist examined me he told me that damage was done to my right eye and as a result there was bleeding into the eye. Also as a result of the trauma, the pupil of my eye was left in a fixed and dilated state. It was unknown whether the pupil would return to its normal size so in the interim it would cause me photosensitivity. An eye patch was placed over my right eye for several days to reduce strain and light from entering the eye.

I was on standby for surgery, which meant that I couldn't eat or drink anything, the intravenous would keep me hydrated and I had a Foley catheter in place to drain my bladder.

On February 14th I was taken to the operating room for surgery on my right leg. The surgeon performed and O.R.I.F. (Open reduction with internal fixation). An external fixator was inserted. This involved two large screws into my lower tibia and two screws into my femur, which were then tightened to the large exterior hardware extending from just above my knee, down the length of my leg to the ankle. My leg was swollen, bruised, difficult and heavy to move and so very, very painful. My saving grace was that most of my time was spent sleeping and when I was awake I was so sedated that I had visual hallucinations and was unable to carry on any form of intelligent conversation.

* * * * *

H. Anne Sinotte

At the time, I could not distinguish what was reality and what was fiction. I remember being very frightened of the "visions" I "saw" and I could not formulate my thoughts constructively to articulate my "visions" to others. It got to the point that I didn't want to close my eyes for fear of what I would see.

Some of my "visions" were flashbacks of the accident. These flashbacks would always be the same, there was no variation and the content was painfully real. I would see myself snowmobiling on the trails then an enormous tree would be looming in front of me, I would be panic-stricken, then I would awaken with a start, still not able to remember the moment of impact. These flashbacks of the accident would continue to haunt me frequently and with every recurrence, I mentally withdrew further into myself in an attempt to block out the disturbing images.

I often experienced other traumatic hallucinations such as drowning and suffocation. These were incredibly disturbing because I pictured myself alone and no matter how loud I screamed or made noise I was unsuccessful in summoning any help, my fate was doomed or so I imagined!

H. Anne Sinotte

I also believed that the hospital heliport was outside my bedroom window. I remember telling Randy and my youngest son Brad about this. They tried to assure me that I was wrong, but when they realized my strong pre-occupation on the subject, they eventually humoured me to avoid upsetting me further. In retrospect, I'm sure the heliport image was a direct result of a subconscious memory of being airlifted by helicopter to the hospital.

The tragedy in all of this is that everyone derived pleasure over my bizarre mental state, while I wrestled with the fears of mental images that were real in every way to me. Perhaps in a way that was a good coping mechanism for those closest to me.

* * * * *

A few days later on February 19th, I was taken to the operating room again for hand surgery. The surgeon performed an open reduction and internal fixation, which involved the placement of screws and plates in my hand. This time when I awakened following surgery I was in the Intensive Care Unit and my right hand was cast from my fingers to just below my elbow. It was necessary for me to be in the unit because my breathing was compromised causing oxygen saturation levels to drop to dangerous levels. I required constant observation that was only possible in the unit setting. The nurses in I.C.U. were absolutely wonderful to me. I remember complaining that my hair hadn't been washed since being admitted to hospital and this made me feel unclean. That night the nurses pulled together some equipment and they washed my hair. I was so grateful to them for this kind gesture especially since they had many more important tasks to carry out during their tour of duty. The following day I was discharged from intensive care and returned to my hospital room.

Unfortunately, when I arrived back to my room on the orthopaedic unit, the nurses were somewhat concerned that my return was premature as I still exhibited breathing difficulties. The nurses attempted to have me transferred back to intensive care but the intensive care doctor rejected their attempts. As a result, they monitored me closely for the next several hours until I showed signs of becoming less short of breath. My condition may have stabilized sooner if I had been compliant with leaving the oxygen on my face. The nurses, Randy and my other visitors were frequently instructing me not to remove the oxygen. I'm the type of person who is easily irritated by anything touching my nose and the tickling flow of the oxygen coming from the nasal prongs was a constant irritant to me.

* * * * *

On February 22nd, 2006, I was taken to the OR once again...three surgeries in nine days. As confused and disoriented as I was, my medical knowledge took over cautioning me that I may be receiving too much anaesthetic in such a short period of time. As a rule I don't handle anaesthetic well...I tend to go into an extremely deep sleep which takes me a prolonged time to come out of, as well as my blood pressure usually plummets after an anaesthetic. Funny enough I seem to remember informing the doctors about this so I could only assume that the amount of anaesthetic I received was calibrated accordingly. Besides, all along I was so heavily sedated that I wonder if anyone would have known the difference if I was slow to awaken in the recovery room.

I remember waiting all day to be taken to surgery and couldn't help but wonder if it would be postponed to a different day. Sometimes it felt like I was on a roller coaster, I didn't know if I should feel exhilarated or deflated.

Finally, I was taken to the OR and it was very late

in the day when I was positioned on the OR table. The anaesthesiologist went through the now familiar routine with me. He administered the medication in my IV tubing, and then had me count backwards from 100, 99, 9………..

I woke up in the recovery room in excruciating pain. My right leg felt like it had been twisted, crushed and put through a vice. I was screaming and writhing in pain. I asked the nurses to let me see Randy and they did for about 30 seconds. When I saw him standing over me I asked him to plea with the nurses to put me out of my misery. I looked at one of the nurses and begged her to give me enough drugs to end this misery. "Please just let me die," I remember saying. At this point Randy was asked to leave because I was out of control. I overheard one of the nurses speaking on the telephone, obviously to the doctor, explaining to him how overwrought I was with pain. She even related to him my comment about wanting to die. Within moments she was at my side administering more analgesic and probably a sedative as well to me to calm me down.

*****

Whatever the nurse had given me in the recovery

room must have been effective, because I was back upstairs in my room. The unit nurse was checking me and asking me on a scale of 1-10 with 10 being the most severe, what my pain level was. I remember telling her it was probably about an 8. She told me that she would give me something more for pain so that I could hopefully get some sleep. I was grateful for this and did manage to get a few hours of sleep.

During the course of the next few days, the pain decreased little by little each day. I was weaned from IV injections of analgesic, to the pump to oral analgesics. There was always pain; the difference was that now the pain was being managed more effectively.

Since the day of surgery there was a gradual improvement daily in my physical status. The nurses got me out of bed initially once a day, then twice a day as I became stronger and could sit in a chair for longer periods of time. I was far from being better but was certainly on the right road to recovery.

I was later to learn from the surgeon what was done in this last surgery. My tibia was completely shattered so the surgeon reconstructed my tibia with bone fragments. Two rods were placed lengthwise to support the tibia and 18 screws held the tibia together. An external fixator was attached to the undamaged area of my lower tibia with two screws and at the top end by two screws into my femur to stabilize the tibia.

When you think about this, it is quite remarkable how my tibia was put back together similar to the story of Humpty Dumpty. It was no wonder that I had so much pain when I was in the recovery room…the end justifies the means!

*****

The doctors informed me that I would not be having any more surgeries in the very near future. It was now time for healing, recovery and rehabilitation. I was told that an application would be submitted for me to continue my recuperation at a Rehabilitation Hospital. Rehab hospitals would review my application and when a bed was available, at the appropriate hospital for my needs, I would be transferred to that hospital.

When it rains on your parade look up rather than down. Without the rain, there would be no rainbow.
G.K. Chesterton

Chapter Three
Leaving the General Hospital

February 27, 2006, this was the date hospital personnel informed me that I would be leaving The General hospital. The plan was to transfer me to a rehabilitation hospital for further treatment and therapy. After two weeks and two days at The General, I was no longer acute in the critical sense and was therefore deemed stable enough for the rehab venue.

I received this news four days prior to my discharge goal date. At first I didn't think about it much, but, as the time grew closer, I found myself becoming nervous, frightened and totally unaware of what was in store for me.

I wasn't given in-depth preparation for this transition, instead doctors and nurses reassured me that my needs would require the skill and resources that rehab would provide.

The unknown presents itself as a huge threat to most people. My head was swimming with questions, thoughts and what expectations rehab would hold for me. I couldn't get past the idea of what would become of me. At this time, I was still burdened by nightmares and flashbacks of the accident, not to mention that I was still quite heavily medicated, causing me to experience irrational thinking. My state of mind was anything but clear...I felt fragile.

My physical state was extremely compromised. I couldn't move my right leg without assistance. My right hand was in a cast from my fingertips to just below my elbow. My chest was severely bruised in vibrant black and blue colours and movement was hampered because of the fractured ribs. I was plagued by headaches and the laceration above my right eye added to the discomfort. I still had an IV running and a catheter to drain my bladder. Oral intake was still a problem for me, as I had no desire to eat anything. The only way I could get out of bed was with the nurses and physio assisting me. Even when they did this I was so weak that it took everything I had not to pass out, not to mention the excruciating pain I experienced from the movement of my broken and shattered limbs. With all these strikes against me, how was I going to function in a rehab hospital?

The more I thought about this move, the more upset I became. I tried discussing this move with Carol one of the nurses that I trusted and felt comfortable with. She compassionately tried to reassure me. She explained that the staff at the rehab hospital were trained to deal with long-term cases like mine and would have more time to be involved with the day-to-day exercises and physio I needed. She added that my progress would be better monitored and measured at this type of facility.

After listening to Carol's arguments regarding the pros for rehab, I promised her that I would try to approach this upcoming transition in a more positive light. Carol told me that she would help me as much as possible in the next couple of days to make this move less stressful. I thanked her for her efforts at reassuring me, but I sensed that she realized just how frightened I really was.

Over the next few days I received many visitors, my girlfriend Pat, my brothers and their wives and children, other friends, previous co-workers and of course my husband Randy. The days and early evenings were filled with conversation, laughter, and tears and in general an abundance of activity. Many times I drifted into sleep while my visitors were present. Of course this wasn't out of boredom, but instead because I was physically and emotionally unable to stay awake for long periods of time. The sleep and rest I received was helping me to heal bit by bit. I can remember telling my visitors that if they lost me in the conversation, not to feel badly about it, it was just the way things were with me then................so I would continue to doze in and out of various conversations with various people at various times.

Randy was at the hospital every day. Many times I looked at him and could see that he looked very tired and worried. And who could blame him............since the accident he had very little sleep, was eating at different times than usual, spent a tremendous amount of time driving back and forth from Toronto to our little town of Brechin which was a good two to two and a half hours away. After a few days of commuting this way, Randy was able to secure a hotel room close to The General Hospital. This made life somewhat simpler for him as he only went home once or twice a week then, basically to check on the house and clear the driveway of the never-ending snow.

H. Anne Sinotte

Of course neither Randy nor I had been given any kind of prognosis from the doctors. The future was unclear to both of us as to what level (physical and mental) of function I would be left with. Again a very scary thought for both of us. We didn't know what path our lives would take and just how many bumps we would hit along the way.

It was now the day before my discharge from one hospital to another. During my time at The General I received a multitude of get well cards, many gifts and an incredible amount of the most beautiful fresh cut flowers, floral arrangements and plants. My bed was next to the window, so I had the window ledge to display everything. In fact I had more flowers than seen at many funerals …….an incredibly beautiful assortment. At least I could easily see the flowers from my bed, without having to contort my body in to awkward positions. That was a bonus.

The worst part of this was that the flowers could not accompany me to the rehab hospital…it was against the rules. Randy took a few of the arrangements to the nursing station but sadly the remainder of the flowers had to be thrown in the garbage. It bothered me that these beautiful reminders of encouragement

H. Anne Sinotte

from the thoughtful people in my life had to be pitched, as one would pitch the wrapper from a chocolate bar. This latest development didn't do much to escalate my feelings about going to rehab.

That last night at The General was a restless one. Sleep came in small, short intervals and the little sleep I did get was disturbed by bizarre nightmares such as the one that I was under water trying desperately to find someone to take me safely home before the ocean claimed me for its own.

Another nuisance was I had to use the bedpan frequently during the night because the catheter had been removed from my bladder earlier that day. To my chagrin, the movement on and off the bedpan triggered pain in all my injured areas. By the time the pain had lessened to a tolerable level, I had to use the bedpan again. This was a no win situation.

After my night from hell, morning finally came. At least it was no longer dark and the shadows of the night were gone.

The day had arrived, Monday, February 27, 2006. In a short time I would leave this "comfort" zone and head into the unknown.

H. Anne Sinotte

All the fears of leaving The General built up in me again and the crescendo came in the form of uncontrollable sobbing. Carol, my nurse entered the room and witnessed my outpouring of emotions. She sat with me on the bed and held me in her arms. She then said, "Let it all out honey…these tears are long overdue for everything you have been through." With that comment the floodgates opened and it was a long time before the gates closed again. When I finally was able to compose myself, Carol gently reassured me once again that going to rehab was in my best interest and I would be fine after I got through the initial stages of adjustment.

I thanked Carol for the wonderful care she gave me during my hospital stay and especially for the pep talks and words of encouragement, in some of my darkest moments. I remember telling Carol that her compassion and caring spirit defines her as a nurse in the truest form. I think this brought a tear to her eyes receiving such praise from another nurse.

H. Anne Sinotte

> Action is the antidote to despair.
> *Joan Baez*

<u>Chapter Four</u>
<u>*Admission to the Rehabilitation Hospital*</u>

On Monday, February 27, 2006, the ambulance took me from The General Hospital to The Rehab Hospital in the west end of Toronto. Randy followed the ambulance to The Rehab Hospital. The paramedics delivered me to my room and along with two members of the nursing team they safely placed me in my bed but not without me experiencing terrific pain in my right leg during the process. From what I could gather it was still morning probably around 11:00 am. I must have drifted off for a time especially since I slept poorly the previous night. In actual fact, I just wanted to be left alone, to shut out the world and wither away in my own little cocoon.

From what I could see, I would be sharing this room with three other women. My little niche was on the right upon entering the room. The nursing staff introduced me to the other roommates. Two of them were about 20 years my senior and the other one was only about sixteen or seventeen years old. I remember meeting various staff but couldn't retain their names.

Before I knew what was happening I was awakened by one of the nurses. She needed to complete an admission history and profile about me. I remember rushing through her questions and at times I likely demonstrated impatience over this procedure. In actual fact I just didn't want to be bothered with any of this, I just wanted to sleep.

A little while later the physiotherapist assigned to my case entered, introduced herself and completed an assessment of my abilities. She then got me up to the bathroom with the assistance of two other staff. I was transferred by means of a high-wheeled walker. This process caused me an incredible amount of pain and I regretted it every time the need arose. I was told that I would be starting my therapy program within the next couple of days.

It was either on the first or second day at The Rehab Hospital that I met one of the two doctors there. Dr. D. as he liked to be addressed examined me and attempted to take a history but he saw that I was fatigued and decided to finish the history a couple of days later.

H. Anne Sinotte

Pat visited me the day after I was admitted to Rehab. As I spoke to her I started to cry, as I felt so depressed, frightened and alone. The road ahead seemed so long and unknown. She tried to reassure me that everything would work out. She pointed out that my injuries were so severe that it was a miracle I was alive. Pat stayed with me and at lunchtime she encouraged me to eat and even tried to feed me, but I had no appetite and felt nauseated most of the time. I also felt feverish and indeed did have an elevated temperature. Pat remained with me until I drifted off to sleep.

Within two days my therapy had started. At first therapy consisted primarily of strengthening exercises for my unaffected left side and upper body. It was important to do this in order to compensate for my impaired right side. At first these exercises exhausted me to the point that I had little tolerance or energy left for anything else in my day, but as time passed my tolerance increased along with my energy level.

I had a student nurse assigned to me for the first couple of weeks. This was a real treat. In the mornings she assisted me with getting washed and dressed. One day she and one of the nurses washed my hair, which was no easy task, as my hair was long and the process had to be done with me in bed. The student was wonderful to me. At mealtimes she assisted me into a comfortable position to eat and she opened containers and cut up the meat for me. Even though I still had a very small appetite, she prepared the tray to encourage me to eat. Unfortunately, there was a strike in the community colleges, so that was the end of having a student nurse.

Activities of daily living now became much more difficult. The nurses rarely offered me any help. I don't know if they expected more from me because I was a nurse, but if so that was not fair as I was a patient like any other in the hospital. The lack of assistance from the nurses made the daily challenges I faced paramount.

In the mornings I virtually got washed and dressed without assistance from the nurses. This was very frustrating because it took every ounce of determination and energy to complete this task, energy that I needed to perform physiotherapy exercises. Many days I cried behind the curtains surrounding my bed.............I felt so abandoned and helpless.

H. Anne Sinotte

After I was dressed the nurses would transfer me out of bed for the sole purpose of making the bed. Usually I went to therapy around 10:30 am for about an hour. Upon returning from therapy it would be lunchtime and I seldom ate because I was too tired or I needed assistance with meal set-up, but didn't receive any.

I basically ambulated by wheelchair and required someone to push me in the wheelchair. This routine continued for several weeks and my left leg and upper body were definitely showing signs of becoming stronger.

* * * * *

Throughout my stay at Rehab, I had to return periodically to The General Hospital for follow-up appointments. Initially, I had to be transported by ambulance because of the status of my right leg. Following these appointments I would be very tired. This was a lot of activity and visual stimulation for one so ill.

Three weeks after arriving at Rehab, I had the cast to my right hand removed at The General Hospital. Once the cast was removed, I couldn't believe what I saw. My right arm had lost all of its mass of muscle and fatty tissue. My forearm looked similar in size to that of a starving child. It left me with a sick feeling in my gut. During this visit I also had the sutures in my right hand removed as well as the sutures and staples in my right leg. I tolerated most of the procedure okay except for the sutures in my hand. They were embedded and difficult to remove. I was so distraught that one of the paramedics held my good hand in an effort to comfort me. It was at this appointment that one of the surgeons in the fracture room discovered that I developed a right drop foot. Just what I needed...another problem.

When I returned to Rehab the follow-up report was reviewed and a foot cradle was obtained for me. I had to wear this cradle at night when I was sleeping to act as an aid for decreasing the foot drop.

During my four months at The Rehab Hospital, I had approximately 10 return follow-up trips to The General Hospital. These appointments were with the various surgeons assigned to my case, for tests. I also had appointments with an Occupational Therapist who was registered in hand therapy.

One visit with my hand surgeon was to remove three pins that were stabilizing my right baby finger. This procedure was not painful or uncomfortable. It was at this appointment that I got a really good look at the extent of injuries to my right hand. I was astonished at the surgeon's ability to reconstruct and save my baby finger, even though there was no movement at all from the baby finger. Instructions were given to me to take back to Rehab to begin gentle passive range of motion to my right hand.

On another visit to The General Hospital two months later in April 2006, the external fixator was removed from my right leg. This procedure had caused me some worry for several weeks because I knew I wouldn't be sedated for the removal of the huge screws inserted in my leg bones. On the day of this procedure the doctors at The Rehab Hospital gave me extra sedation to take prior to the removal. Now it was time, so I took a deep breath and looked into the faces of the four or five hospital personnel surrounding me in the fracture room cubicle.

First the external hardware, screws, and bolts were removed. This just left the four screws that extended into my tibia and femur. Along with my nursing background, my curiosity was peaked as I watched the first screw slowly being twisted like a corkscrew from my lower leg. Suddenly I felt the blood drain from my head and I could sense that I was going to faint. One of the attending nurses, who knew I was anxious about this procedure, took one look at me and realized my fate. In a matter of moments she brought me a glass of water and put a cool compress on my forehead. At this time the surgeon distracted me so that I couldn't watch the procedure any longer. It seemed like an eternity, but finally the last three screws were removed...and I was relieved.

The procedure was not painful...it was more uncomfortable than anything else. What bothered me the most was the idea of how the screws had to be removed? Following the procedure I was given a splint to wear that extended from my ankle to mid-thigh. This splint was intended to stabilize my leg and also to assist with ongoing healing. I was given instructions for Rehab for passive exercises to stretch my Achilles tendon, which would decrease further progression of foot drop.

On yet two other visits to The General Hospital, the hand therapist made me two splints. Watching her do this was an education in itself, as she explained each step along the way. The first splint, called a static splint was to be worn at night. This splint kept the fingers extended for hours at a time. The second splint referred to as a dynamic splint, was to be worn several times during the day, with a gradual increase in the length of time worn. This splint focused on flexion of the fingers, especially my fourth and fifth fingers. At rehab therapy time would be increased significantly to accommodate these exercises.

The whole worth of a kind deed lies in the love that inspired it.
             The Talmud

Chapter Five
Gruelling Rehabilitation

Therapy sessions were gruelling at best and of course some days were worse than others. Achieving success with therapy depended widely on many factors including; receiving adequate sleep at night and rest periods during the day, taking analgesics before pain was too intense and also prior to therapy, one's emotional state of mind and preoccupations, one's physical state…having other bodily functions working properly, the moods of the nursing staff…many of whom could be quite testy, whether one had visitors recently, and so on and so forth.

It was so amazing to witness the effects any of these factors had on one's performance. The effects could be crippling and exhausting. Getting through therapy each day required a clear mind and a willingness to persevere. Without a positive attitude there would be little improvement in physical function therefore, no growth as a person.

There were many such days for me during rehab and for various reasons; pain, other physical body complaints, depression, sadness, lack of energy and on occasion I was known to hold my own "pity" party. At these times I physically was unable to function productively. These setbacks affected me both physically and mentally and escalated my depression. When I had a day like this, the key was to put it behind me in order to work harder the next day. A little voice in my head reminded me that if I wanted to return home, I had to be able to carry out activities of daily living in a safe and more independent manner. So as a result, I pushed myself and worked harder than most to improve.

Hand therapy became more aggressive. The fingers on my right hand were pulled, extended and flexed at each joint; my wrist was twisted and turned to the point that I cried out with pain during every session. The therapy was so intense and uncomfortable that I literally writhed and wriggled in my wheelchair, praying for the session to end. Other patients watched me with difficulty and could only imagine my pain. There were even a couple of big, strapping young men who refused to stay in the therapy room when this was happening, because

H. Anne Sinotte

they felt sorry for me and the pain I was enduring.

After some time, a different form of hand therapy was introduced, in hopes of reducing pain. My hand was dipped three times into hot paraffin wax, and then wrapped in wax paper and a towel for ten to fifteen minutes. After this time, I peeled off the hardened wax and moulded it into a ball, which I would then squeeze, concentrating for the most part on using my damaged third, and fourth and fifth fingers. After doing that for a few minutes then the rehab aide would do passive range of motion to my hand, wrist and fingers. The wax treatment initially took the edge off the pain, but by the end of the session I was beside myself once again in pain.

Months later when my hand therapy was performed by an occupational therapist, then eventually by a physiotherapist, I was informed that the hand therapy I received while at the rehab hospital was much too aggressive and could have had a negative effect on my outcome.

As noted in the previous chapter, I was referred to a hand specialist at the General Hospital. This specialist made a hand splint with elastic bands that could be adjusted. These elastic bands would then be used to flex and extend my fingers therefore increasing the range of motion to my fingers. The splint was applied several times a day for about an hour each time, so the flex I obtained was gentle, gradual and constant. This was when I started to notice some improvement with the use and function of my right hand.

Rehab, it didn't matter how one felt or what was taking place, rehab was never cancelled. There were days that I could not hold my head up because I was so tired but I was still dragged down to the rehab room.

I remember my first day; my rehab consisted of getting up to the washroom on a platform walker. The entire procedure seemed agonizing. I just wanted it all to be over so that I could get back into bed. All I could think about was sleeping...that is all that mattered to me. It became clear that I was not going to win; there was no way I was getting out of doing therapy. My attitude really sucked at first, as I felt really sorry for my dilemma and myself. It was around this time that I realized I had to make some attitude changes. It became clear to me that I had two choices. I could either bury my head in the sand and forget about doing anything to help myself or I could pick myself up, shake myself off, then get on with life, improving my quality of life and physical abilities to my highest potential. I chose the latter. I have never been a quitter, I have been a survivor all my life and I wasn't about to stop now. Today my life was going to change for the better. I will improve immensely and I will walk again. My decision made, it was uphill from here on in.

I had a wonderful, compassionate rehab aide whom I will rename Lois. The two of us clicked upon meeting and developed a successful therapeutic relationship. Each day we trudged through the various exercises and routines but the routines became more a labour of love. Lois pushed me and I wanted to please. I wanted to not just get through therapy but also excel with it, so Lois and I moved forward. She always pushed me a little beyond my limits and I accommodated her requests.

At first the focus of rehab was strengthening exercises and balance. My upper body was targeted as a priority. I worked on it daily two or three times because I needed my upper body for positioning and lifting my lower body. I even did therapy in my room when in bed as I watched my roommates sleep or talk with their visitors. I just kept thinking of the end result. For the first two to three months, I even had therapy on the weekends. At first I found this difficult as Randy often came in early on a Saturday morning and stayed the entire day. I was reluctant to give up my time with him, but he understood that this was all in my best interest.

I also had a student rehab aide for the first few months at the rehab hospital. As with Lois, Donna and I also developed a great relationship and became quite close. She was the type of girl I would have loved one of my boys to be involved with. At the completion of her placement, she made a beautiful scrap booking card/plaque, which she presented me with. I was so touched as it was a thoughtful, special gift that I would always treasure. This made some of the tough times all worthwhile.

Physical therapy was getting better week-by-week and I was getting stronger and with increased strength I was regaining a modicum of independence. This meant the world to me because independence promotes self-esteem, something I have been lacking since the accident.

Friends who visited early in my admission noticed great gains on my part after a couple of months, proving to be a positive reaction for them as well. They could see the Annie they once knew trying to poke through again.

H. Anne Sinotte

I couldn't believe how strong my upper body was becoming, as well as the improvement in my balance. I still had an external fixator on my right leg so this put limits on what I could or could not do with my lower body. Instead of dwelling on what wasn't working I forged ahead with what I could do and concentrated on doing that stuff as well as I could.

Eventually in April 2006 on one of my return visits to the General Hospital my external fixator was removed. What a treat it was to not have all that hardware in my leg and to be able to move about more freely. As I discussed before I watched the procedure of removing the hardware until the first screw was removed. At that point I became weak and almost fainted. The procedure didn't hurt; it was more the point of watching the hardware being unscrewed from the bone. The nurse started me on some oxygen and within a couple of minutes I could feel the colour returning to my face and I no longer felt faint. The fracture clinic attendant was able to resume the removal of the other three screws. I chose not to watch the last three screws being removed and I was better off for this.

Once all the screws and hardware were removed it felt weird to no longer have all that stainless steel

H. Anne Sinotte

attached to me. I was so used to protecting my leg from being jarred or hurt especially when someone else was pushing me in the wheelchair or assisting me with a transfer. I was always afraid of doing damage to my leg. It felt bare without all this hardware protruding from my right side. I wonder if I will experience some sort of phantom attachment issue like when one loses an arm or leg.

Within a few days after getting the external fixator removed, one of the physiotherapists Teri approached me about starting hydrotherapy. The thought of doing some exercising in the pool was very appealing so towards the end of April 2006, I commenced pool therapy in the therapeutic pool...I loved it! Teri, the physiotherapist in charge of pool therapy was absolutely amazing. On my first day a lift was used to lower me into the pool. This was a little frightening being suspended in air but I got through it with the help of a few deep breaths. I was a little overwhelmed by everything and being in the lift made me shaky. I was so afraid of the lift malfunctioning and crashing into the pool. It doesn't matter whether I am in the car or any other moving object, I'm constantly afraid of an accident occurring. Thankfully the lift didn't crash and I was slowly lowered into the pool. Teri spent the entire hour putting my right knee and hand through range of motion while submerged in the inviting warm water. The buoyancy of the water made the exercises tolerable and almost soothing compared to the agony I usually experienced. I had a peaceful feeling when I came out of the water, almost like there was a light of hope surrounding me. Teri informed me that I would be having pool therapy three to four times a week. I was elated with this news and couldn't wait until the next session. At the end of the session Teri had me bend my knee and she measured my flexion at 70 degrees…WOW…this was an excellent improvement.

The following day my elation over pool therapy was short-lived when I discovered a red area on my lower right leg. It was shiny, warm to touch and painful. I feared that I developed a cellulitis, which is an infection in the tissues. I marked around the area with a pen so I could observe for further spread of the infection, and then I showed it to the nurse. On Dr. D's next rounds he addressed this concern and agreed that it likely was a cellulitis and therefore I would be started on antibiotics to treat it. He told me I could continue with pool therapy as long as I covered the area with opsite, which is like a medical saran wrap. His recommendation pleased me immensely, so much so that a few tears escaped.

H. Anne Sinotte

Movement became easier the more I was in the pool. After a couple of sessions I was able to sit on the stairs of the pool and "bum" my way down the stairs in to the water. Once in the pool, Teri gave me specific exercises to work on to strengthen my legs and arms. Exercising in the pool felt wonderful due to the buoyancy of the water. There were not the usual aches and pains of being on land to perform these exercises. I was able to move so much more freely. I felt if I stayed in the pool I would make such progress because my pain was reduced.

I continued with pool therapy until I was discharged from hospital. I made great progress with this form of physical therapy and would recommend it to any one, especially people with injuries as severe as mine. Teri was great and it was clear that she loved what she was doing. Her positive attitude overflowed to her patients and we all benefited from her expertise. Pool therapy was definitely one of my best experiences while in hospital. I looked forward to this daily therapy, it made me feel alive again with some purpose and normalcy in my life.

The remainder of my stay in rehab, I spent at least

H. Anne Sinotte

two hours a day in supervised therapy. This involved passive exercises to stretch my Achilles tendon, workouts on the parallel bars, bed exercises, hand therapy including; paraffin wax treatments followed by passive range of motion to my hand, fingers, and wrist, and walking with a walker with a right arm trough. Weight bearing on my right foot was gradually increased as healing progressed. I also spent at least another two hours in my room with a self-directed therapy plan. While in my room, I worked with thera-putty to increase strength in my hand. I also used other aids (balls, games etc) to work the small muscle groups thus promoting function in my hand. I applied and wore the hand splints and foot splint as directed. There were many times when I struggled for long periods trying to apply the foot splint. This activity was difficult for me, but when I asked the nurses for assistance most of them were reluctant to help me. I couldn't understand their reluctance, but eventually a few nurses engaged themselves to lend me a hand. I realized that there were only a couple of them that actually understood the proper way to apply the splint. In the end, I relented and did it myself.

I did other strengthening exercises for my upper body and unaffected left side and practised walking with the walker at every opportunity. With this regime it left very little time to rest or relax and I found myself being exhausted frequently.

H. Anne Sinotte

So long as we are loved by others I should say that we are almost indispensable; and no man is useless while he has a friend.
Robert Louis Stevenson

Chapter Six
Emotions Soar

By the time May 2006 rolled around I was on an emotional roller coaster. One moment I was smiling and laughing and the next moment I was in tears. I just couldn't get a grip on my feelings no matter how hard I tried. I think I could sense myself sinking further into a depression. Looking back this was around the time that the reality of my condition started to sink in. I had been so heavily sedated to this point that it was difficult to separate reality from fiction, like the nightmares I was having.

My world had been condensed to my little eight foot by eight foot cubicle hospital corner, going to the physio room and the therapeutic pool for therapy. I had no concept of what was happening beyond these confines and in retrospect I don't think I even cared. All that seemed to matter and that I could concentrate on was my little world. How sad, this all seemed for an individual who previously had a caring, and unselfish demeanour.

I say that nothing mattered but in fact everything mattered. Every aspect of my recovery depended on everything else. It is difficult to explain but my performance in physio was directly affected by my emotional state. My emotional state improved only when I made physical advancements. Pain was intensified by lack of movement, depression, flashbacks and malfunctions in normal bodily functions. What a catch-22 this all was and dealing with these struggles on a daily basis was extremely challenging. Some days I wanted to scream at the top of my lungs that I didn't deserve this and life wasn't fair, but that wouldn't have accomplished anything, other than relieving some stress? Yet at other times I felt sad, defeated and just wanted to be left alone to die. This isn't a pretty picture, but it was in fact my reality.

Emotions were affected by lack of sleep and privacy. Sometimes my other three roommates didn't sleep, so inevitably I didn't sleep. Events in their lives indirectly affected my well being. If any of the roommates faltered with their progress, I became engulfed in their disappointments, as these people were my "family" now...we were all enmeshed in each other's lives. If one roommate had a bad day, we all had a bad day, when one experienced joy, we all experienced joy. The average person could not begin to understand this concept because it had to be experienced.

Dealing with staff was another major concern. I got to know most of the staff quite well because of the length of time I was in hospital. For the most part I had a good rapport with most staff but then again I did not ask them for more than I had to. I guess the nurse in me was too proud to ask for help, and to be perfectly honest there were some nurses who wanted to do as little as possible to help the patients.

The staff consisted of registered nurses, registered practical nurses, physiotherapists, occupational therapists and rehab aides. Most of this list of staff was excellent in what they did and how they did it. As in any other work venue there were a handful of mostly nursing staff that left a great deal to be desired. Professionalism, empathy and caring were some of the attributes lacking with this minority. On occasion patients were spoken to inappropriately, ignored or spoken down to. This form of abuse caused much discontent amongst the patients, many of who were afraid to defend themselves due to repercussions in their care. Most of these patients were elderly and didn't want to rock the boat.

I often wanted to intervene on behalf of various roommates but knew that it wasn't my business or that my roommate advised against it. I found this entire ordeal frustrating to say the least. I would not accept abusive behaviour from my staff or myself in my nursing practice, so this was most uncomfortable territory. This matter disturbed me to the point that I sat down with the nursing coordinator prior to my discharge to discuss these concerns with her. I emphasized that this only applied to a limited number of nursing staff. The bulk of the staff was very supportive and we as patients looked forward to them being on duty. My intent was to improve the quality of care provision by having the coordinator re-evaluate her staff and educate the staff on how they are perceived by patients. What they could improve on and what they do well. It is like any other system, feedback is required to affect positive change, which will in turn allow growth and development.

One of my biggest frustrations was getting assistance to put a foot drop splint on my right foot. This splint was recommended by the surgeon to be used whenever I was in bed. In the daytime the RA (rehab aide) would put it on for me, but when I asked for assistance to put it on at bedtime, I was given excuses such as; "I don't know how to apply it", "I'm busy at the moment but will come back later", Usually later was once I'd fallen asleep, so inevitably the splint did not get put on. After several refused attempts I stopped asking the nurses and struggled immensely to put the splint on by myself. Once I had it on I was exhausted, sweating and my back ached from overstretching to reach my foot.

None of the staff offered to wash my back or my feet. In fact the only time these areas got any attention was when I had nursing students assigned to me. The students treated me with such dignity and respect...this was pure heaven. Unfortunately, the teacher's strike caused an interruption for a few weeks in student placement. Most patients like me who had students assigned to us were deeply upset when this happened and we sure missed the undivided attention we received from the students.

I think back to when I was first admitted to the Rehab hospital, I was physically and emotionally "battered". My right leg was immobilized by an internal fixator, making it difficult to move around

H. Anne Sinotte

and reposition myself in bed, my ribs were fractured causing my chest to be severely bruised...black in colour, which made my breathing laboured...I was still receiving oxygen, my right hand was in a cast from just below my fingertips to my elbow, so I had no use of this hand. My head pounded constantly from the head injury I sustained and vision from my right eye was obscured. I couldn't think straight, was weepy and could care less about what was going on around me. Yet when it came to mealtime (meals were served in our bedrooms) the staff did not offer me assistance with opening containers, cutting food or general meal set-up, or positioning me to eat. As I am right handed, even feeding myself with my left hand was a major chore at that time. Inevitably, my meal tray would be removed untouched with everything exactly the same as when it was first placed in front of me. There were no questions asked such as; "Are you not hungry? Was there something wrong with the food? Is there anything wrong?, Are you not feeling well?, Is there something I can do to help?". The staff robotically went about completing their tasks, they delivered the meal trays then removed them at the end of the meal...their job was done...not correctly to my standards, but nevertheless done. In the beginning the only nourishment I received was when either Randy or my friend Pat happened to be there over a mealtime.

There were two separate incidents when my back had gone into spasms, rendering me incapable of getting in and out of bed without assistance for a few days. Every movement left me in agonizing pain, so I summoned help only when absolutely necessary. I sensed the staff's reluctance to help at these times because of the length of time it took me to get from point A to point B, but we got through it and my back returned to its normal state.

One would get the impression that the staff were all monsters, from the accounts I have given but that just was not so. Yes there were some miserable, uncaring nurses, but there were also some wonderful, compassionate, dedicated nurses as well. These were the ones that sometimes came to my room for no reason other than to chat with me for a few minutes or to comfort me if they knew I was upset, or to scold me for not taking analgesics or working too hard in physio. These were also the nurses who took the extra time to wash my hair because they knew it would improve my spirits. Then there was the nurse who spent the better part of the morning with me trying to get my bowels to function after approximately six weeks with limited function. Her tedious efforts were rewarded with a

H. Anne Sinotte

positive outcome. Then there was the nurse whose eyes lit up the first time she had seen me after the external fixator was removed from my leg. The nurse who cried with me when I found out I was finally being discharged from hospital.

Oh there were some great nurses and I applaud their diligence and caring dispositions. I hope that they will always remain the positive caregivers and uphold the true essence of nursing practice.

The longer I remained in hospital the more I wondered if I would ever return home. This was apparent as I watched so many roommates and other patients being discharged. At times I felt like I had seniority because I was there longer than most. I inevitably played the role of the welcome wagon as well as the bon voyage well wisher. I just wanted to be "normal" again, to be at home with my family and friends, to watch television with my husband and sleep in my own bed and look around at my personal belongings...it seemed like a dream.

H. Anne Sinotte

You cannot do a kindness too soon, for you never know how soon it will be too late.
Ralph Waldo Emerson

Chapter Seven
More Tragedy

The phrase "if it doesn't rain, it pours", can be applied to so many life experiences, including death.

In April 2006 while I was in the rehab exercise room I was summoned to the telephone for an important phone call. I answered the phone to hear my older brother Steve's voice. He called to let me know that my Uncle Charlie had passed away. Tears flowed immediately causing me to choke up to the point that I could barely get any words out, so I ended the call. My Uncle Charlie was my favourite. He was one of the kindest, compassionate and most humble individuals I have ever known and I loved him deeply. His death would be a huge loss to many people.

I was not strong enough physically or emotionally

to attend visitation or funeral services for my uncle, so I had my own little dedication to him at my bedside. I reminisced about past times with him or when our families were together and I paid tribute to his many acts of kindness and how I was a better person for having him in my life. My brothers and their wives attended the arrangements for Uncle Charlie and shared with me an account of his funeral and interment.

* * * * *

In May 2006 while still in hospital my sister-in-law Tracy passed away suddenly. She had only been in hospital for about a week. She had a virus that attacked her heart and there had been talk of her being put on the heart transplant list. Unfortunately, she threw a fatal blood clot to her lung. I learned afterwards that at the same time that Tracy died, I was sitting at my bedside praying for her to hang on in hopes of receiving a transplant.

The next day, I was having hydrotherapy when I was informed that I had visitors waiting for me. After hydrotherapy I got showered and dressed and wheeled my wheelchair to the waiting room to receive my guests. I looked up to see Randy and my sister-in-law Angie. I panicked then retreated to the change room. In my heart of hearts I knew they came to deliver bad news to me about Tracy. I went back to the waiting room and they told me Tracy had died. I felt numb at first but then my thoughts went to my brother Mike and to his and Tracy's young sons, Travis and Trevor. In light of Tracy's sudden death, this must have been a devastating time for the three of them. Tracy was only 46 years old.

This was a very upsetting time for me because I felt helpless. I wasn't able to help my brother with any of the arrangements, or to help look after the boys for him or do anything.

The doctors at the Rehab hospital agreed that I needed to be with my family at this time, but due to my fragile state I was only allowed to attend one visitation session and the funeral. When I attended the visitation it was overwhelming in many ways, primarily because of the sadness of Tracy's premature passing and watching the devastation and emptiness in my brother's face and my two nephews who were lost because their mom was taken from them. Another challenge was seeing all my relatives and other people that I hadn't seen since before the accident. It was difficult finding the strength to repeatedly reassure everyone that I was

H. Anne Sinotte

okay and improving. I didn't want this time to be about me, it was about Tracy, Mike, Travis and Trevor. The next few days were difficult finding closure and saying goodbye to Tracy, as she was laid to rest. Now all we can do is pray for Mike and the boys to eventually find peace.

* * * * *

In June two days after I was discharged from hospital, there was yet another death in the family...my sister-in-law Hazel's mother Barbara. Although Barbara's death was expected, it was sudden. One week after my return home from hospital we went back to Toronto for Barbara's Memorial service. I remember feeling so tired at this event and almost like I wasn't there. People don't realize that when someone is wheelchair bound they forget to talk to that person on their physical level, therefore the person feels excluded from most conversations. It is very degrading for the disabled person and it makes that person feel even more handicapped than necessary.

* * * * *

I felt like the challenges presented so far in 2006 would never end...it has been a continuous battle

H. Anne Sinotte

and the battle is not over yet. Even though my mental function, thought processes were temporarily decreased, I couldn't help but notice unsettling changes with my dad. He was showing definite signs of dementia and these signs were manifesting very quickly. At the time dad was living with my brother Mark. Mark would tell me things that dad would do that were inappropriate for the situation at hand, the visual and audio hallucinations and general safety concerns regarding activities of daily living. The situation was progressively getting worse to the extent that dad required twenty four hour care, seven days a week.

A family meeting was held early in the summer, with my three brothers, our spouses and myself. I informed my brothers that it was time to start the process to get dad into a long-term facility. At first there were mixed feelings about this but I pointed out to my brothers that this process does not happen overnight so we needed to initiate matters before dad's needs were intensified. Once everyone was in agreement, our next step was to discuss long-term placement with dad. This was not something any one of us was looking forward to doing. On the chosen day we all met at Mark's house and it was decided that I would be the spokesperson as this was my area of expertise.

H. Anne Sinotte

After I carefully addressed the matter to dad using specific examples demonstrating the need for long-term placement, I asked dad if he understood what I was saying to which he responded affirmatively. Then I asked him how he felt about the situation and he stated that he agreed with us 99%. I was so relieved with this outcome but was also very proud of dad for realizing this was the best solution, to meet his needs.

Dad was admitted to a long-term facility just before Christmas 2006. Unfortunately, dad's mental function deteriorated quickly as the dementia escalated. There were times when I visited him that he didn't know who I was and my brothers also experienced this. It was so sad to see dad lose his grip on reality. At times he was in his own little world. Dad remained at the long-term care facility until his death on November 27, 2007. He had a major stroke that lasted less than 24 hours before he was at peace with his maker. My family were all present for his final day and in many ways we were relieved that his suffering was over and he would be reunited with mom.

H. Anne Sinotte

We deliberately waste time only with those we love ~ it is the purest sign that we love someone if we choose to spend time idly in their presence when we could be doing something more productive.
            Sheila Cassidy

Chapter Eight
Going Home/Facing The Real World Again

It was June 8, 2006 and I was being discharged from the physical Rehab hospital. The day I had been hoping and praying for had finally arrived but so had many mixed emotions. For months now I had been confined to my little eight foot by eight-foot cubicle in the hospital. Most things I needed were within my reach. My meals and snacks were prepared for me and brought to my bedside for me to eat. Nurses set up basins of water at the bedside for me to wash or took me to the shower room and assisted me as needed. I received in- house physiotherapy and occupational therapy. I was taught and shown how to get in and out of a vehicle. I only had to go downstairs in the hospital to have my hair done by a hairdresser. The podiatrist attended regularly and performed treatment to my feet right at the bedside. The psychologist also came to see me and would take me to a private room to provide therapy. I was in a protected world with supervision everywhere and safety and comfort measures all around me. It wasn't going to be anything like this at home, it would be the complete opposite, a world of reality opening up to me to rediscover.

It was time to say goodbye to life, as I knew it for so many months now. I made the rounds by saying goodbye to other patients, exchanging phone numbers, saying goodbye to nursing staff, physio, and occupational staff, housekeeping and custodial staff and of course the medical personnel. I left goodies for all the staff that Randy had purchased for me and now it was time to go. I had been given discharge instructions, several appointments to follow-up with and of course prescriptions. I was told that an occupational therapist would be meeting me at home shortly after I arrived to complete a home care assessment of my needs.

As Randy was pushing me in my wheelchair away from my sanctuary, I couldn't stop crying. I was so frightened, sad and almost feeling indifferent about everything. We made it to the parking lot and with Randy's help I was able to negotiate getting into the car.

We then took the two and a half hour journey home and even though I was in pain it felt good as I took in the familiar scenery that I had not seen in months, during the drive home. Once we pulled into our driveway the challenges started. I was able to dismount from the car into the wheelchair without much difficulty but then the next obstacle was climbing the garage stairs, which entered the house. The procedure took twenty minutes to complete. This is where I saw my physical weakness and disability take hold. I could not grip the handrail on the stairs to pull myself up the stairs with my forearm crutch. Eventually, when I caught my breath I sat on my rear end and backed up the stairs on my bum.

When I entered the house I was blown away...everything seemed to be so large and spacious. Upon looking around our floor plan I realized how fortunate it now was that we designed our house in an open concept style. This style would accommodate my movements in a wheelchair and walker without having to manipulate my way around too many walls or separate rooms. I looked around the remainder of the house and was stunned when I entered our master bedroom. Our king sized bed was completely covered with my clothing that Randy had laundered, a multitude of gifts I had received while in hospital, greeting cards and various support aides and braces. The bed would have to be cleared at some point in time before I retired for the night, but certainly not at this moment because I was just too tired and overwhelmed. I returned to the living room and parked myself on the sofa and drank a cup of tea that Randy had made for me.

It was now two o'clock in the afternoon when the doorbell rang. It was the occupational therapist arriving to complete an in-home assessment of my needs. We chatted briefly about the accident, the surgeries and treatments I had undergone, present and future therapies, treatments and surgeries. After obtaining this history, now it was time to proceed to present and future needs. The O.T. (occupational therapist) put me through a slew of range of motion exercises, she observed me using my walker, my ability or lack of for bending, sitting, rising to a standing position, getting in and out of bed, getting in and out of the shower, climbing stairs etc. She checked my grip strengths and ability to life objects. She asked me questions regarding what duties I carried out in the house prior to the accident, so that she could determine what duties I would now require assistance with.

I was becoming so very tired that I just wanted to sleep but the assessment was still ongoing. Eventually after five long hours the assessment was finally complete. The O.T. had arranged for a Medical Supply Company to come to our house the following day to deliver items I would require to assist me with daily living. Also equipment installations would be done where deemed necessary.

I don't mean to sound unappreciative for all he O.T. did for me but I was so relieved when she left our home. I needed to re-adjust to my surroundings and how I would adapt with my present disabilities. I sensed it was going to be a tough road ahead.

The next few days I spent acclimatizing myself to being at home and the challenges that go along with that. I didn't talk a great deal, as I was just content being thoughtful of my whereabouts. Arrangements were being made to get me started on physio for my leg, OT for my hand and an assessment with a psychologist. Just using the phone and booking appointments was an ordeal for me because I had not used a phone much in the past five months.

H. Anne Sinotte

During the first week that I was home, I started receiving in-home physio for my right leg because it was just too difficult for me to get out of the house to a clinic. On my physiotherapist's first visit (I'll name her Julie) she amazed me by being well-versed about my accident, the injuries sustained, treatments done and ongoing treatment required. I remember thinking how refreshing it was to not have to reiterate this entire experience again. Julie saw me twice weekly at home for the first month. She worked out an exercise program for me to do by myself three times per day. When she attended me she worked on more intense stretching of my leg and ankle. This regime worked well but after a month Julie found it necessary for my treatments to be shifted to the clinic level. At the clinic the treatment beds had the firmness required to facilitate the stretching needed plus there was other equipment such as ultrasound, which would be accessible to me.

When July rolled around I was going to the hospital twice a week on Tuesdays and Thursdays for OT of my right hand and having my hand splint checked and adjusted as necessary. Following OT I would then go to the physio clinic for my right leg therapy.

I was so impressed with Julie and the regime she set

up for me. She worked conscientiously to improve function in my leg and right hand. By the beginning of July she was able to remove the right arm trough from my walker and she worked with me to get me using the walker in a normal manner. She was now able to use almost full body pressure when trying to stretch my leg to increase extension. There had been noted improvements with flexion at my right knee as well as extension, even though extension is more difficult to achieve and maintain. Julie made ongoing suggestions for new exercises, therapies and treatments to improve function to my limbs. She made great strides using ultrasound and range of motion to increase the movement of toes on my right foot and specifically the great toe. Although these therapies can be very uncomfortable, I knew they were necessary if progress was to be achieved.

In September 2006, I stopped going to OT at the hospital on a routine basis and would follow-up only as necessary if problems arose or if my hand splint required adjustment. Julie had taken over my hand therapy and continued to be diligent in improving function of my right baby finger. My fourth finger has improved well and I can now use it as part of my handgrip once again. There have been subtle improvements with the baby finger and I am now trying to use it more by incorporating it in with

H. Anne Sinotte

my hand movements.

Having one less appointment to attend was a nice change not only for me but for Randy as well, because it was one less place for him to drive me to while juggling his work schedule.

I no sooner lost the OT appointment then gained appointments with the psychologist. At my first session the psychologist completed his initial assessment of me and then set up regular sessions to discuss the concerns related to Post Traumatic Stress Disorder and Depression. These sessions were helpful to me because I was able to open up with a trained professional and also it made me think about the accident, my injuries and circumstances related to it. The sessions allowed me to vent concerns, anger and fears while exploring ways to deal with all of this in a healthy, healing manner.

My biggest obstacle when attending sessions was the physical layout of the building. There was no elevator in the building only stairs. Unfortunately, the only way I could negotiate the stairs was by going down backwards, so this also added to my stress level.

H. Anne Sinotte

Our therapy sessions continued for about one year. I was able to sort through many emotions during that time. The most important tool was just having someone listen to me without interruption or being judgemental.

When I wasn't attending physio or psychology appointments, I had numerous medical appointments at the downtown Toronto hospital. Appointments were scheduled with several leg surgeons at the fracture clinic, the hand surgeon, neurologist, psychologist and neuro-ophthalmologist. It seemed that there was never a week that we weren't trotting off to Toronto. Of course these appointments were so tiring because of the travel and time spent waiting to be seen by the appropriate source. However, I quickly came to realize that these were all stepping-stones to my recovery.

Some of the challenges encountered since being at home are quite remarkable. Loss of independence and the ability to carry out routine household activities such as: cooking, cleaning, laundry etc. This is difficult at best as my disabilities prevent me from actively completing these tasks.

Since coming home in June, I slowly paced myself

to assist with these tasks but specifically cooking and laundry. One huge hurdle was not being able to go outdoors without assistance due to stairs and the equipment needed. Randy built a deck outside that is accessible from the main floor level of the house. This allowed me to be able to go out on the deck by myself with the aid of my walker.

Another challenge was being shut-in staring at the same walls day in and day out. Having the deck reduced this feeling slightly as I was able to get out and breathe some fresh air.

One of the biggest challenges was not being able to drive, therefore, having to depend on someone for all transportation needs...to take me to physio twice weekly, the psychologist weekly, to follow-up appointments in Toronto, to do groceries, go to the hairdresser etc. This was extremely frustrating for me because I had lost control from my previous high level of independence. Randy transported me everywhere and this upset me because I knew he was very tired from all the extra chores/tasks he had to inherit. At times I felt like I was more of a burden to him.

There are also so many simple aspects of activities of daily living that were no longer simple for me.

H. Anne Sinotte

Just getting myself washed, showered and dressed every day was exhausting. Then I had to get myself something to eat. At first, this was awkward for me, as I could not carry any items because I needed my hands to manipulate the walker. It usually took me about 20 - 30 minutes just to organize a bowl of cereal and a cup of coffee. By the time I got everything ready I was too tired to eat it. The O.T. ordered a tray that rests on the walker so that I could place items on the tray while walking to my destination. This made life a little easier. Sometimes just walking from one end of the house to the other end tired me easily and of course I experienced pain in my right leg if I was on my feet for any length of time.

Other challenges included finding time and energy to do my exercise program three times a day, apply JAS ankle brace three times a day for 30 minutes each time, apply and wear my hand splint three times a day for one hour each time, do hand therapy with theraputty once a day for 30 minutes, wear my foot cradle daily for two hours and twice a week attend physio and once per week my appointment with the psychologist. This left very little time for me to do something for leisure such as knitting or reading a book, but I came to the conclusion that my treatments were my full-time job and everything

H. Anne Sinotte

else would be re-introduced into my life when progress was made with my recovery. Patience, patience, patience!

I was so grateful for Randy and the ongoing support he gave me. Without him I do not know how I could have gotten through this ordeal. He gave me strength to get through each day.

The fall-out from this type of accident does not only affect the injured person but also close family members and friends. I'm fortunate and grateful for all the players in my support network.

H. Anne Sinotte

A little kindness from person to person is better than
a vast love for all humankind.
Richard Dehmel

Chapter Nine
Handicap Resources

It was probably as a result of my change in physical status that I became more aware of the handicap resources available to people afflicted by disabilities. The more I was faced with imploring the appropriate resources, the more my eyes were opened and the angrier I became. People with physical disabilities have enough challenges to overcome every day without dealing with the lack of handicap resources or the improper use of resources.

This became so apparent to me as I now had to access many of the resources myself. One of my first experiences was so awkward that I cried for sometime afterwards. I was in a wheelchair with my right leg elevated on a leg-extender trying to access a handicap washroom in the hospital. I pushed the button that should have automatically opened the door to the washroom in an inward fashion but it was not functioning, so now I had to propel myself in the wheelchair so that the back of the wheelchair was against the washroom door Then I had to use my good hand, the left one to turn the handle on the door enough that I could then propel the wheelchair backwards pushing against the door until I was safely in the room. By the time I had done all of that I was exhausted and needed to rest for a minute before I did what I went into the bathroom for in the first place. Of course as luck would have it, there was a knock on the door. The person waiting on the other side of the door didn't see the struggle I went through to get into the washroom in the first place. I let the person know that I would still be a couple of minutes. When I had to exit the bathroom the struggle started again. This time I wheeled myself out frontward's with one hand self-propelling the wheelchair while keeping my right hand holding the door open. Once outside of the washroom I lost any feelings of guilt for taking so long when I realized that the person waiting to use the washroom had no visible physical reasons for using the handicapped washroom. This annoyed me because I had rushed and in doing so could have caused further injury to myself over someone who was capable of walking to a regular washroom.

H. Anne Sinotte

Public washrooms that just have a larger stall for wheelchair accessibility are the biggest nightmare. First of all the entrance doors are quite heavy making it very difficult to enter. Once inside it is problematic manoeuvring the wheelchair into the handicap stall. One has to avoid hitting other people with their wheelchair, getting the wheelchair into the stall, then find enough room to safely transfer from the wheelchair to the toilet. It makes one think twice about using public facilities, not to mention all the stares and whispers from onlookers, throughout the experience.

I remember at my sister-in-law's funeral, two other women having to assist me in getting into the washroom and into the handicapped stall, due to the tightness of the room. I probably could not have attempted this on my own.

I think one of the most misused areas and one of the most troubling to me is disabled parking. I don't know how many times I have seen people pull their cars into a disabled parking spot without having a disabled parking permit displayed in the window or on a visor or license plate. The unfortunate thing is they get away with it because there is no one around to enforce this. All one can do is telephone the

H. Anne Sinotte

police with the license plate number of the person in violation, but by the time police would get there the person could be gone. This is so troubling as the disabled person who truly requires nearby parking usually then has to park an inconvenient distance away and often struggle to get to their destination.

Once when I was at a shopping mall in Florida, I pulled into a disabled parking spot. My disabled permit was clearly visible in the front window of my van. As I was about to leave the van a parking attendant checked my permit and gave me a thumbs up...that is the one and only time I have seen this law enforced.

There are so many types of equipment needed by people with physical disabilities and each type of equipment presents with its own challenge. The injuries I sustained in my accident left me with many physical deficits which most "normal" people would consider quite limiting. I remember the frustration I felt getting from point A to B and knowing that for most forms of ambulation, I needed someone else to assist me, whether it was from wheelchair to bed, wheelchair to car or just general positioning. It is a terrible feeling having to depend on another person for so many of your physical needs. Sometimes I avoided any changes just so I didn't have to ask for help.

Originally I started my journey in a wheelchair with someone pushing the wheelchair. This probably lasted for about two and a half months until my right hand was healed enough to self-propel the wheelchair. Once able to self-propel the wheelchair I gained a tiny bit of independence which allowed me to venture out on my own a little more. At first I tired easily self-propelling the wheelchair but after a while I developed upper body strength which made all the difference in carrying out this task. Ambulating with my wheelchair was the most common method I used for getting around, however, the rehab staff also worked closely with me to teach me how to ambulate with a wheeled walker. This was somewhat challenging at first, as I could not weight-bear on my right leg. I essentially pushed the walker forward then moved my left leg forward while my right leg remained flexed and away from the floor, much like the manner in which an amputee would move. This also required a great deal of upper body strength to manoeuvre my walker in this fashion. Using the walker proved to be more practical for getting in and out of the bathroom. It wasn't as big and clumsy as the wheelchair and much easier to manoeuvre in a small space. As time went by I figured out which piece of equipment was most appropriate for my need at that time.

I must say that when one is in a wheelchair you almost feel forgotten by the rest of the world People tend not to talk to you or if they do talk to you they talk down to you instead of lowering themselves to be at the same level. I found this very frustrating to the extent that when I spoke to people, I often was not heard. I could not imagine having to go through this every day of my life. I made a promise to myself that whenever I would speak to someone in a wheelchair I would place myself at eye level to that person, out of respect for that person.

The next challenge I had to face while in the rehab hospital was learning how to ascend and descend stairs. This posed huge problems for me. First and foremost, I was frightened of falling especially since I couldn't weight-bear on my right leg. I first learned to climb the stairs using my rear end and keeping my bad leg extended forward, but eventually I would have to learn how to do this in an upright position. It was decided that the best and safest method for me would be with the aid of a crutch with a forearm trough attached for my right arm. To ascend the stairs I put the crutch on the stair immediately above me, my left hand would be holding the handrail firmly while pulling my body upwards, my right arm would be pushing down on the crutch until I was safely on the next step. To descend the stairs this procedure would be reversed. This took many sessions of practice before I felt confident that I could attempt this on my own. I even learned how to descend the stairs backwards in the event that the handrail was on the opposite side for my needs. Every staircase would be different and I would have to attempt each one accordingly. It was entirely different using the same staircase every day in the rehab hospital so little did I know how much more difficult it would be coming home and climbing the stairs from my garage into the house. Until smaller handrails were installed on the existing larger handrails this task was impossibility for me, as I couldn't properly grip the previous handrail safely because my hands were too small. Slowly and patiently I was able to accomplish this task with confidence.

As I mentioned previously, when I returned home after spending five months in hospital an Occupational Therapist came to my home to assess what home modifications would be required to meet my physical needs. In my bathroom the glass doors were removed from the shower stall and replaced with a shower curtain, a pole from ceiling to floor was placed beside the shower to assist me in getting in and out of the shower. A hand held shower was installed so I could sit while showering and rinse myself off. Also a bath seat was provided for getting into the bathtub and it could also be used when sitting in front of the mirror for my grooming needs. A grab bar unit was placed over the toilet to assist me in getting on and off the toilet more easily.

In the kitchen, a cutting board with a knife attached was devised so that I could chop foods with little risk of cutting myself. There was also a tool to help me, which attached to a dish in the oven then made it easier to pull that item out of the oven.

I had a "reacher" to assist me with obtaining difficult to reach items, a tool that helped me put my socks on, a long handled sponge to help me wash my feet. I had a walker with a carrying bag as well as a tray, which enabled me to carry a drink or a plate of food from point A to point B. This was a great tool. I also had a rollator walker for outdoor use; it had a seat on it so that I could rest when I felt tired or weak. Of course I also had a wheelchair, which I required for most appointments and out of home functions. Eventually, I acquired a scooter, which made day-to-day living more tolerable. This

H. Anne Sinotte

scooter allowed me to get outside more and go for a spin around the block or go to the mail kiosk to access my mail. I was grateful for this independence.

All the equipment and tools I acquired and used helped me significantly in getting through the many obstacles and dilemmas faced by the disabled every day. Fortunately for me I overcame many of the disabling effects caused by my accident through hard work, determination, good physiotherapy from an excellent therapist and a good support network of people encouraging me to succeed. Not everyone is this lucky. Some people have always been disabled or will remain severely disabled for the rest of their lives. These are the people that I empathize with because the challenges are many and they are tiring, frustrating and often insurmountable.

Although handicap resources have been addressed and great strides have been made to improve tools and make safer controls and resources for the disabled, there is still much needed to increase the dignity of our disabled population and bring them to a level of equality. Much of this could be achieved by ongoing education to the public through advertising, commercials etc. The public needs to know what they can do to improve the quality of

H. Anne Sinotte

life of the disabled, even if just to look someone in the eyes when speaking to them, or assisting a person to negotiate a physical barrier or not parking in a disabled designated spot without a government permit. These requests may seem trivial to the average person but they are paramount to persons with physical disabilities.

H. Anne Sinotte

With a friend at your side, no road seems too long.
Japanese Proverb

Chapter Ten
The People I Love

While I was in the General Hospital I received visits from family friends and ex co-workers. These visits went a long way in making me feel loved and appreciated. Unfortunately, my condition was critical and I was so sedated that I could not truly enjoy the many conversations that took place. The important thing was that people cared and did not desert me in my time of need. The floral tributes, other gifts and cards I received were absolutely astounding. The window ledge was filled to capacity with flowers of every colour and variety. On a couple of visits my dear friend Pat had to create space for more arrangements by mixing flowers from different vases together. It was a shame that with so much beauty around me I could not fully appreciate it or the generosity of all those who sent the flowers. I do however remember thinking how blessed I was to have so many thoughtful people as my support network...there were other patients who were not as fortunate as I was, in this respect.

I love teddy bears and have accumulated quite a collection over the years. People who knew this about me brought me more teddies to add to my collection. I received strawberry and chocolate scented bears, a bear in a hospital gown, a large cuddly one, a beautiful bear made especially for me of fur and another one made for me by my young niece Kristyn...this one is so cute, dressed in a pink outfit and across the front reads, "Lucky Duck". It actually wasn't until I came home that I could really look at these bears and enjoy them and appreciate the thoughtfulness of the gift givers.

One of my goddaughters, Erin gave me a beautiful angel figurine that she informed me was to be my guardian angel to watch over me. Erin felt so strongly about this gem that she purchased one the same for herself. In the months to follow Erin decided to get a tastefully done tattoo of one aspect of the figurine. She told me that I inspired her to do this as a result of my courage in this latest crisis. I remember thinking...how extraordinary, that a 17 year old would have this kind of insight.

During my almost five month hospital stay, I

continued to have many visitors but as time went by the number of visitors decreased, partially due to the location of the rehab hospital and the lengthy distance most people had to travel to get there. Randy came often and Kev and Brad came when they could. Some of my friends and brothers continued to visit pretty regularly. One of my sister-in-laws, Angie would cut my finger and toenails whenever she visited because I was unable to do so. My friend Lynn would always take me for a walk, in my wheelchair of course, inside the rehab hospital when the weather was not so great and outside the building during better weather conditions. This helped to give me a change of scenery, as well as allowing me to breathe some fresh air into my lungs. I always looked forward to these visits and cherished our time together.

My dear friend Pat was a constant figure in my life and throughout this ordeal. From the time she heard about my accident until present she has been one of the key players in my support network. She has been one of my rocks from which I gathered strength to face each new day and carry on. I don't think that she was aware of the value of her presence, the true difference it made in helping me stay focused on what I had to do to get better. I guess you could say that Pat gave me purpose...purpose to do the best possible to make myself feel somewhat whole again...the road to finding a way back to being me once more.

As I have stated before, much of my stay at the general hospital remains a blur to me, so the facts are not clear. Pat was at my bedside at various times of the day, depending on her work schedule and what was happening with me. Pat's face was often the one I saw prior to surgery or upon waking after surgery. Many times she sat quietly in my room beside my bed, reading a book, grading papers for school or just resting, while I slept. Her vigil was unrelenting. This following statement may seem odd in the sense that even though I couldn't always see Pat, I knew or sensed that she was there. It is almost comparable to being twins. Our bond is so strong that we have an uncanny connection to what the other person is thinking and feeling.

There were times in the early stages of my hospitalization that I was so depressed, add that on to the severity of my injuries, I couldn't see what I had to live for any more...too much of my life was taken from me. I wasn't eating much and had no desire to eat but Pat would come in at meal times to try to get some nourishment into me...sometimes this meant feeding me. My weakened state only allowed me to consume the tiniest amount of food, just enough for a bird to eat.

I knew that initially Pat was concerned about various after effects of my head injury, mainly my slow, slurred speech, memory impairment, thinking impairment and use of words and word finding. It bothered Pat to see this diminished capacity in my mental function, but that didn't stop her from helping me to regain or improve this function. Pat would keep written notes for me with dates of all my surgeries and who the surgeons were, special appointments or dates of significance, if a noted improvement was made or I took my first step or moved my big toe, she had it all documented. We spent a great deal of time together...healing time. I will never forget everything Pat gave me, all the time she shared with me, time she should have been with her own family. I will cherish these memories always.

Other key players during this time were my friends Lynn and Paul. We had been friends for about twenty-one years at the time of my accident. I am godmother to their daughter Erin and I provided day care for their older son Kevin when he was a baby and in the toddler stage. I love this family and have felt their love as well over the years.

H. Anne Sinotte

Lynn and Paul had quite a distance to travel to visit me in hospital; first at the general hospital in downtown Toronto, then afterwards at the rehab hospital in the west end of Toronto. They lived about 100 kilometres east of the greater Toronto area and yet they came to visit on a regular basis including after all the numerous surgeries I had Their presence would cheer me up and leave me with a warm feeling inside.

Sometimes Lynn would take a half-day off work to visit me. Usually she chose a bright sunny day that she would be able to take me outside in my wheelchair to get some fresh air. I enjoyed these walks and the great talks we had as well...it was our special time. I remember one visit towards the end of my stay in the rehab hospital; the occupational therapist took Lynn and me out to the parking lot to her SUV as she wanted to demonstrate the proper method for me to get in and out of the vehicle...much needed experience for my discharge home. Lynn was so enthused about being a part of this, seeing the proper way to transfer and to assist me with it. It impressed me that Lynn was so connected to being a part of my care. The three of us practiced vehicle transfers and after about thirty minutes I felt comfortable with performing this

H. Anne Sinotte

procedure.

There were many other visits from Lynn. Sometimes, Erin came with her and one time Katherine, Lynn's daughter-in-law to be accompanied her. Lynn's son Kevin was getting married at the end of July 2006, so on these visits I would get to hear about the wedding plans at whatever stage the plans were at. It was a sort of therapy for me discussing something other than my injuries and health status. Actually Lynn was so sure that I would be dancing at Kevin's wedding but I look back to that time I think she was just trying to keep things as positive as possible, as encouragement for me to continue to improve...she did that a lot!

During my quiet times in the hospital I remember thinking how blessed I was to have such good friends who did not desert me because the going got rough; instead they supported me through the many trials, disappointments and challenges. This truly defined the meaning of friends.

One of the women I worked with in Whitby was another constant at my hospital bedside. Jackie would visit often and bring other staff members with her. This could always perk me up seeing different people, talking with them and even sharing a little humour at times. It helped to make my world more "normal" again. It seemed that every time Jackie came to visit she brought me another cuddly bear. She was the one who gave me the strawberry shortcake bear that smelled like strawberries and a dark brown bear that smelled like chocolate. Jackie did whatever she could to lift my spirits and let me know that I was loved.

Unfortunately, about a year after the accident I stopped hearing from Jackie and I knew she had changes taking place in her life that required her time and concentration. I could accept that because I believe that each person who enters our lives does so for a reason and Jackie's reason had been fulfilled.

Mark, my youngest brother would bring my dad to visit me in the hospital. Many times I saw tears in my dad's eyes. He did not know what to think of my condition, nor what to say to me, so he often remained quiet.

My life was changing so quickly. Many times I lay in bed crying and wishing my mom were still alive to talk to and have her comfort me and tell me everything would be okay. In my heart of hearts I

H. Anne Sinotte

think I knew that she was watching over me and directing my care, even guiding me to persevere through all the difficult, painful therapies, to achieve a more desirable outcome.

This experience brought to light who my real friends were. There were many people who initially showed concern but backed off with the reality that I would remain disabled or just weren't there for me when I most needed the help. This was apparent when I came home from the hospital.

We had our current home built a few years earlier and it is a couple of hours north of Toronto and about one and one quarter hours north of Whitby where we previously lived. We didn't know many of our new neighbours because Randy and I still worked and commuted back to Whitby and Toronto. We had no friends in the area and I had no family in the area either. Randy had several aunts and a brother living not too far from us, but for some reason Randy's aunts thought we didn't want them around. This of course was not true. Randy had asked that initially upon my return home from hospital that we be given some time and space to get re-adjusted to the many changes in our lives.

Of course I found life very challenging without

assistance. There was no one to make me a cup of tea or coffee, a sandwich at lunchtime, help with the laundry, preparing meals, cleaning and tidying the house, do the outside maintenance such as lawn cutting, weeding etc. It was an extremely difficult time for both Randy and me and at first Randy had to do most of these tasks. As everyday life became more and more difficult we asked Randy's mom to come and stay with us for a couple of weeks to help out. This was wonderful just having someone else in the house in case I slipped in the shower or to help prepare meals or just assist me with activities of daily living...what a God send Trish was. She also came to stay with us in the future after two other surgeries I required.

I know had I still lived in Whitby, I would have received assistance from various sources, but that was not meant to be as circumstances changed. In some respects, I think this was just another reason for me to overcome as many of my physical obstacles, so that I could once again function with some of the independence I previously enjoyed.

H. Anne Sinotte

We are given dreams a size too big so that we can grow into them.
- Author Unknown

Chapter Eleven
Breakthroughs and Baby Steps

I am overwhelmed when I reflect back to February 2006 and recall the extent of my injuries. The physical injuries, which affected all of my movements, caused significant challenges for me to overcome, but the emotional and mental issues probably had a greater impact in the whole scheme of things. My thinking process was greatly impaired along with decision-making, speech, memory and word finding to name a few.

During my 5 month stay in hospital the rehab I received was mostly physical. Much of the training I received was strengthening my upper body to compensate for the lack of movement on the lower right side of my body. My upper body became relatively strong and I depended on it to raise myself up and for repositioning, especially when in bed.

H. Anne Sinotte

Hand therapy was a very important aspect of my care. Once the cast was removed and the sutures removed, then therapy was started. It was intense and painful. In the beginning my fourth finger and baby finger stuck straight out. It didn't seem like these two fingers would ever bend again and because they stuck out everything got caught on them or they were prone to injury. Eventually, I started to get some flexion back in these fingers. This gave me some encouragement that all the pain and hard work was finally showing some improvement.

As discussed, for months my right leg was immobilized in an external fixator, which had screws extending from the fixator into my tibia and femur. Once the fixator and screws were removed, therapy to my leg included strengthening exercises, exercises to straighten my leg because the knee was contracted, and foot exercises to treat the drop foot. The drop foot developed as a result of the immobilization of my leg for such a long period of time.

One of the biggest breakthroughs I had was movement of my right great toe. I remember how excited I was the first time I was able to move my big toe. One of the doctors was doing rounds when she asked me to try to move my toe. The movement was so slight and painful to achieve but none the less a baby step in the right direction as there was nerve damage to this leg. As it turned out I did not regain much more movement in my big toe. The nerve damage was too severe for the nerve to regenerate. I would have to accept what little movement I presently had.

As physiotherapists and physio aides continued to work on all my physical areas of concern, I was determined to tackle my mental and intellectual deficits. I tried doing word puzzles to jog my memory. I thought just seeing various words would trigger my memory to make bringing forth these words an easier task. I also took time to meditate and let my mind wander to past events. In doing so I was sometimes able to piece together past memories especially events from the not so distant past. When I was alone I would pull the curtain around my bed and practice speaking while holding a mirror in front of me. Gradually my speech improved to the extent that I spoke faster and used words in an appropriate manner. Word finding is improving but to current day still remains an area of weakness for me.

H. Anne Sinotte

I eventually asked to be referred to the Head Injury Clinic at the General Hospital, but this was months after my accident. I had several tests done at the clinic and was referred to a psychologist. After a couple of visits with the psychologist he booked me for a full day of psychiatric testing.

This day of testing was exhausting. I didn't understand some of the tests and the examiner was not permitted to explain some tests to me...they were interpretive tests with common elements but I wasn't always able to determine what the common element was. At the end of the day I was not only exhausted but also frustrated that I didn't do better with some of the testing. Things that I knew, I missed...I felt so stupid, so inadequate. Weeks later when I returned for the results of the testing I once again became overcome with feelings of inadequacy. The psychologist told me that there were areas affected as a result of the accident. A speech pathologist was one recommendation for me. He also diagnosed me as P.T.S.D., Post Traumatic Stress Disorder and Depression and suggested that I continue to see a psychologist to help me work through these problems.

Once again another baby step...psychological testing indicated that I was above average in most aspects, so all my fretting and feeling frustrated was unnecessary.

Looking back I am so grateful for all the breakthroughs and baby steps gained from hard work and determination to improve and get better. I started off in the General Hospital being bedridden and could only get out of bed with the assistance of three other people. I progressed from that point to a wheelchair with a leg extension for my right leg. I required someone to push me in the wheelchair, as I was unable to perform this task for several reasons. After doing this for a couple of months I then learned how to self-propel myself in the wheelchair. I was in a wheelchair for many months as I was not able to weight-bear on my right side. Eventually, I learned how to use a walker weight-bearing on my left side only, as I kept my right leg suspended in the air. This was not easy because it required a great deal of upper body strength. I ambulated in this manner until June 2007, after having surgery to reduce my right knee contracture and remove hardware from my right tibia. I was now able to weight bear on my right side.

Once I became comfortable weight bearing and using the standard walker I graduated to using a rollator walker outdoors and the standard walker

H. Anne Sinotte

indoors. I used a forearm crutch for climbing stairs because my right hand wasn't strong enough to grip handrails. Presently, I am able to walk with a single cane. I think this is a pretty great feat considering the doctors initially thought my right leg might have to be amputated and that I would never walk again. These baby steps ended up turning into a huge leap for me.

As far as my mental state I still experience some memory deficits such as not being able to recall some details of incidents from the past. Decision-making has improved however it takes me longer to process thoughts in order to make a decision. By far word-finding still remains my biggest mental challenge, but I continue to push myself to find the word I'm looking for that best defines the context of the material. The most noted mental improvement is my speech. Enunciation, speed and clarity have returned which makes having a conversation not just a more pleasant experience, but also less frustrating for me.

H. Anne Sinotte

A good friend is cheaper than therapy and much more fun.
- Anonymous

Chapter Twelve
Let's Try Surgery Again

In 2007 after I was home from the hospital for almost a year, I had to return to the General Hospital for more surgery on my right leg. Originally, I was supposed to have three procedures done, a manipulation of my right knee which would reduce my knee contracture, removal of hardware from my right leg and my Achilles tendon was to be snipped which might help my drop foot. As it turned out only the first two procedures were necessary.

I was only in hospital for a day and a half, but the pain I experienced was knawing like it was going through the bone. There was a brace I had to wear on my leg, which helped to keep the leg extended. I found the brace to provide support, so much so that when I took it off my leg ached more, and therefore, I wore the brace as much as I could.

When I returned home I had new therapies and equipment to use. It was like being back to square one again. At first for about two weeks my physiotherapist came to my house to provide therapy because of the amount of pain I was in and the difficulty I was having getting around. We worked at keeping the knee contracture reduced but the reduction did not last long. Within a couple of weeks the knee contracture had returned to its pre-surgery state of lacking full extension by about twenty-seven degrees. This was so disheartening but in actual fact the contracture likely would not improve until a total knee replacement was done and the orthopaedic surgeons were not yet prepared to do this.

For months I continued therapy trying to do everything possible to maintain the level of function I came to know. I was ordered a special splint called a JAS splint which stands for Joint Activation System, to place on my ankle three times a day for thirty minutes each time, to provide stress relaxation and static progressive stretch to my very stiff ankle. I used this device for four months from September 2006 to February 2007 and it did help to loosen the movement of my ankle. Along with all my other therapies and exercises I had to do using this device certainly filled in the rest of my day.

H. Anne Sinotte

I also had a foot positioner that was applied when in bed. It was to help with the drop foot, which was a result of nerve injury. This foot positioner was not easy to apply by myself but many times I had no choice so I applied it as best as I could and I kept it on for as long as possible. It stretched the foot while pulling the foot forward. My tolerance for wearing this depended on many factors including pain, anxiety and even mood. As time went by I used the positioner much less.

A nerve conduction study was booked for me at the General Hospital. The initial part of the test was okay but the latter part was terrible. The neurologist stuck long needles in various parts of my body. I found this not only invasive but also very painful...painful to the point that the test had to be stopped.

The neurologist informed me that there was definitely nerve damage to my perineal nerve. She indicated that nerve damage appeared to be originating from a higher source possibly the lumbar region. Her questioning regarding injury to my back at the time of the accident left me somewhat curious as to whether this was a possibility. Later at home I read the ambulance report. The paramedics stated that while attending me I had frequent complaints of pain in my lumbar region. The neurologist did not seem too hopeful that nerve regeneration would take place and if it did the effects would be minimal.

I realized that all the time I invested in trying to move my right foot and toes up and down, would be probably to no avail. Real movement was just not going to happen. Even now five years later I have no more movement in my right foot than I did four years earlier.

H. Anne Sinotte

Ah, how good it feels. The hand of an old friend.
  Henry Wadsworth Longfellow

Chapter Thirteen
Decreased Quality of Life

In 2007 I found myself becoming more and more depressed. I was experiencing decreased quality of life due to constant, severe pain in my right knee, difficulty weight bearing on the right side and the inability to straighten my right leg. Getting around was so bewildering for me that it restricted me from going places; shopping, visiting friends and family and generally having fun. It was like my life was on hold. Every return visit to the General Hospital had the same outcome. The orthopaedic surgeon would examine me, book tests and arrange to see me again in another six to eight weeks.

At one of my appointments towards the end of 2007, I totally lost control of my emotions and frustrations with one of the orthopaedic surgeons. I think I shocked him with my response to the point that he listened more intently to my complaints. I cried a river that day, all the pent up anguish, anger, frustrations and pain poured out of me, just looking for someone to listen to me and understand my pain and help me to move forward with whatever adjustments were necessary. I relayed to the surgeon in no uncertain terms that I wanted to have the knee replacement now and not in another couple of years. I explained as best as I could that until the surgery was done my quality of life would not improve and getting around was so difficult for me especially to carry out any form of normalcy in my life...after all I was only 55 years old.

The knee orthopaedic surgeon was a little reluctant to move ahead with the knee replacement but I do believe that he was empathetic to the fact that my life was basically stagnating, and I was still a reasonably young woman. He ordered another x-ray of my right leg and knee and reviewed the pros and cons of doing a total knee replacement at this time. He then agreed to do the surgery in January 2008, so this was only about four to five months away. This would allow me to get through Christmas then start the New Year with some increased hope for a more complete recovery.

* * * * *

Christmas 2007 came and went and now I was

focused on the preparations for my surgery. I had the usual pre-op work to do; signing the consent for the procedure, pre-op blood work, urinalysis, cardiogram, chest and right leg x-rays, history and medical and I also had to attend the viewing of a video on knee replacements. When all the prep work was complete, it was just a matter of waiting for the operating day to be admitted to hospital.

The night before surgery Randy and I drove to Toronto and stayed in a hotel so that we wouldn't have as far to travel the day of surgery, considering we had to be at the hospital for about five or six o'clock a.m. That evening we went out and had a nice dinner, but I found myself quite preoccupied and nervous about the pending surgery. In actual fact a week or two prior, I had written letters to Randy, Kevin, Brad and a couple of my dear friends just in case I didn't make it through surgery, or if I developed complications of surgery. I wanted each one of them to know the important impact they had on my life and how blessed I felt to have them in my life.

I didn't sleep well that night, too many nagging thoughts.

The day had finally arrived, Wednesday, January

23, 2008 and Randy and I were en-route to the hospital. Once we arrived at the hospital he dropped me off while he went to the parking garage, and I slowly made my way to the surgery admission wing and got myself registered. Randy had returned and was once again at my side. We were seated for a short period of time, and then I was called to the reception window, gave the information asked for, after which I was escorted to the pre-operative prep room.

In pre-op, the first thing I was given was a hospital gown and slippers to change in to. Upon return; after the nurse verified pertinent info about me including: allergies, date of birth, next of kin, etc. and an intravenous was started and a Foley catheter was inserted into my bladder. Afterwards the anaesthesiologist came and spoke to me about how everything would proceed. He asked me if I preferred a general anaesthetic or a spinal block with light sedation. I opted for the general anaesthetic as I do not do well with spinals and have on occasion had untoward effects as a result of the spinal. He also offered me a block injected into the groin area, to be initiated after the general anaesthetic. The purpose of this is that it has a numbing effect and would assist in pain control from the knee replacement for approximately 72 hours. I agreed to this as I thought reduced pain might be a great way to start the recovery process, post-surgery.

Shortly after the anaesthetist left I had about five minutes to talk to Randy, then the OR staff came to transport me to the operating room. Once in the operating room everything progressed quickly. I was given the anaesthetic and my next awareness was waking up in the recovery room. Through blurred vision I saw my surgeon and I remember him telling me that surgery was a success. I was in and out of consciousness until I awakened in my room, probably several hours later.

I slowly moved my head around the room to take in my surroundings. I was in a room with three other women and the washroom was straight ahead from where my bed was located. I probably would not need the washroom for the next day or so, as I had a Foley catheter in place.

At some point in time that evening I was able to stay awake for about thirty minutes, so I used my cell phone to call Randy. I just wanted him to know that I was out of surgery and holding my own in my hospital room. We had discussed earlier that there was no reason for him to wait at the hospital all day.

H. Anne Sinotte

Surgery was going to take several hours and afterwards I would be out of it. Our conversation was short but served the purpose intended. After speaking to Randy I again drifted off to sleep and did not remember much until the following morning.

I was awakened by activity in the room. My roommates were getting started with their day. I attempted to move and reposition myself in bed but the pain ripped through my leg like a knife, not to mention that my leg felt like it weighed a ton. It was obvious that before I did any moving about, my pain would have to be addressed with analgesics. When the nurse entered the room I voiced my need for analgesic, which she prepared and administered to me by injection. She gave the analgesic a few minutes to take effect, and then she set me up with a basin of water, soap and towels so that I could get washed. The nurse assisted me with washing my back and legs then she wanted to get me out of bed to sit in the chair for a while. This was not an easy task. As I sat at the side of the bed dangling my legs, I felt light-headed and weak. I attempted to weight-bear on my right side but found it too painful, so with the nurse's help I pivoted my way into the chair beside the bed. Now I was just exhausted. This task drained me of all strength. I was content to remain in the chair until I regained composure.

The nurse served me breakfast that consisted of clear fluids. All I could manage was the apple juice and Jell-O. Unfortunately, it was a matter of minutes before I vomited it all up. Now I really felt terrible...I just wanted to get back in bed. The nurse however, had different ideas. She wanted me to remain in the chair and so I did for about two hours. When I finally got back into bed I nestled in and didn't move.

Randy arrived a short while later and stayed with me for most of the afternoon. I slept on and off all afternoon and took sips of fluids in between.

The next couple of days were much the same. The doctors visited daily and on occasion twice daily. My catheter was removed which meant getting up and walking to the bathroom. The doctors removed the large dressing that had been put on my leg in the OR. There was a suspicious looking area on the inner aspect of my knee...it looked like a haematoma and I knew the surgeon was concerned that this could become infected. If that were the case then only God knew what could happen next. I certainly did not need any further complications or bad news. I knew it was up to me to observe for signs of infection, because the nurses did not seem concerned.

For some reason the afternoon and night nurses were very attentive but the day shift nurses were another story. When I rang my call-bell for assistance to get up to the bathroom the nurses would come after the fact leaving me to go to the bathroom on my own. On one occasion I lost my balance and almost fell to the floor. A couple of the other patients tried to assist me but I didn't want them to get injured in the process. It can be frustrating when one tries to be motivated to recover but doesn't get the assistance required to do so safely.

On my third post-op day, I did not feel well. As the day progressed I knew I was developing a fever. I had the nurse take my temperature and sure enough it was elevated and climbing rapidly. I asked the nurse if she would be contacting the doctor to report this development. I told her that he would want this info and he might want blood cultures done. I guess she did not like another nurse telling her what to do especially when that nurse was a patient, so she became defensive. She told me, "we don't do blood cultures here". I thought this to be a little strange

H. Anne Sinotte

and sure enough the surgeon did indeed order blood cultures to be done.

I never did get the results of the blood cultures, which is probably a good sign. My fever subsided within thirty-six hours and my leg remained infection-free.

* * * * *

Five days post-op I was transferred by ambulance to a rehab hospital. This was a different rehab hospital than the one I spent four months in in 2006.

My first impression of the rehab hospital was quite negative. I didn't want to be there, I was quite hungry because I hadn't had breakfast and I just wanted to be left alone. I was taken to a semi-private room...my roommate was an older lady and I just wanted to go home. Just once when hospitalized I would like to have a roommate closer to my age so that we might share some commonalities. I was so sick of hospitals now that I wanted this experience to be over.

As I lay in bed crying, a nurse came in my room to complete my admission. She took one look at me and decided to give me some space. I explained that I was released from the general hospital before I had had breakfast, so now at ten thirty or eleven o'clock in the morning; I was feeling a little hungry. The nurse said that she would order me some breakfast and complete my admission after I had eaten. I appreciated the empathy the nurse had shown me and thanked her for her understanding.

The pain in my leg was almost unbearable and I have a fairly high threshold for pain. The slightest of movements seemed to put me over the edge. I wanted to just stay in bed and not move at all, but of course that was not going to happen...I was on a physical rehab unit, the emphasis was on movement with the end goal being increased mobility with decreased pain.

I knew that I would have to venture out of my room on a regular basis, even if just to use the bathroom. Each room was equipped with a sink for washing and brushing teeth but no toilet or shower. The latter were located centrally on the unit. I would also need to venture out of my room to meet other people especially people closer to my age. My roommate and I did not share much in common. She was almost thirty years my senior, a very well-read lady, but not the type of person I needed close to me to get through this newest ordeal.

H. Anne Sinotte

The day after my admission I met the physiotherapist and the physio aide. I was given specific times to attend physio in the physiotherapy room. The physio aide would come to my room for the first couple of days to assist me in getting to therapy, but beyond that I was responsible for myself.

On the first day of therapy, the physiotherapist took a brief history then proceeded to passively move my right leg to determine how much movement I currently had. As he moved my leg the pain rifled through me. This was going to be and excruciating time.

As time passed by my frustrations escalated. I couldn't help watching the other patients who had knee replacements doing their workouts or when they were walking in the hallway, they were so much more advanced in their progress than I was. They were getting a greater degree of flexion than I was and the movement in their knee was not as tight. On occasion I would start crying in the physio room because I worked so hard and longer hours than most but less improvement to show for my efforts. On one of those particular days the physiotherapist reminded me that my knee replacement was not a typical one due to arthritis or wear and tear but instead due to severe trauma. He told me that he knew I was giving this everything I had and under the circumstances was making great progress. He also told me not to compare myself to anyone else, just continue to do my best. I tried to heed his words and concentrated only on myself. This took some pressure away from me and made my recovery more focused.

Randy could only visit on weekends due to his job, and just about everyone else worked during the week so their visits were also on weekends. This made the weekdays extremely long because I was alone most days. Pat occasionally visited me on weekdays and another friend who I met in rehab two years earlier also visited me a couple of times...these visits were most welcome. I started to become friendly with some of the other patients and this helped to pass the time. We would get together for chats, ride our wheelchairs together down the hall and eventually walk together either with our canes or crutches in the halls. This was actually extra therapy for us.

During my time in rehab I was still smoking so two to three times a day I would wheel myself outside to the smoking area. There were a group of patients who came outside regularly for their smokes...I didn't go out as frequently as most but we would all chat during these times. This also helped to relieve the feelings of loneliness. We called these smoke breaks "inhalation therapy".

It was interesting hearing each person's story. Most were typical, but there were a couple that were heart-wrenching and left me feeling grateful for my lot in life.

The days stretched into weeks at the rehab hospital and I could feel a depression coming over me once again. It was at about this time that I was asked to start in the hydrotherapy program. I was thrilled, as I knew how much I enjoyed this program two years earlier. I would be attending this therapy every morning Monday to Friday and couldn't wait to start. Now I had something to look forward to once again.

Water therapy was great. I could gradually feel my knee joint loosening a little. Not to mention how much less painful it was exercising in the water as opposed to on land. This definitely was a positive step in my recovery. The instructor with authorization from my physiotherapist allowed me to step up the intensity of my program as my needs for greater challenge increased. I could not only see but also feel the benefits of this program.

Around the third week in February I started to become really homesick. Many of the patients I had befriended had been discharged home after a week or two of rehab. This reminded me once again of my previous stint in rehab two years prior, when I watched patients come and go, roommates change regularly, but I remained there, always welcoming new patients or roommates. I hoped that my discharge wouldn't be too far down the road.

My original roommate had been discharged and my new roommate was even more unsuitable. She actually should have been in a room by herself. She was not very motivated and was also up in years. She spent most of her days and nights in bed. A bedpan was used for all her elimination needs and she passed foul smelling gas constantly. It was a nightmare of a time. I was not sleeping at night and didn't get a chance to nap in the daytime. I wasn't eating much due to the air quality in the room. Eventually, I had the nurses serve my tray in the hallway, just so I would get some nourishment. I found myself venturing outside more often to get fresh air into my lungs.

H. Anne Sinotte

Nighttimes were the worst. I would be exhausted from the day's activities but between my roommate's snoring and passing gas I couldn't sleep. One of the nurses brought me earplugs, which helped a little, but I could not get past the odour in the room. It got to the point that I would take my pillow and blankets and lay on a hard wooden bench in the hallway. It was not the most comfortable but it allowed me to get a couple hours of sleep.

I spent very little time in my room, poured everything I had into pool therapy, physio, did extra physio on my own, visited other patients and just generally kept very busy.

Finally at the end of February the doctor asked if I was ready to go home and of course my answer was yes. He had initially planned on discharging me the upcoming Monday but I convinced him to let me go two days earlier on the Saturday. I was ecstatic. All I could think about was sleeping in my own bed for an entire night.

When I found out my discharge date I phoned my physiotherapist to set up some appointments, so that I did not have to wait too long before getting treatment to my knee.

H. Anne Sinotte

The night before discharge I said my goodbyes to some of the patients I developed a relationship with. There weren't too many left, most had already been discharged. I didn't sleep well that night for many reasons and was good and ready to leave the next day. When Randy arrived I gave the nurses some goodies we had purchased for them, picked up prescriptions and discharge instructions and we left. I spent five weeks in physical rehab this time, so I was very anxious to return home.

We made the just over two-hour trip home without event. Neither one of us was talkative, probably because in our own way each of us was exhausted and needed time to chill out. Upon arriving at home I made tea and Randy and I relaxed in our living room for a few hours until it was time to think about dinner. It felt so good to be home again.

H. Anne Sinotte

*When you look at your life, the greatest happiness's
are family happiness's.*
Joyce Brothers

Chapter Fourteen
Onward & Upward

It felt good to be back in my home again. It's amazing just how much you miss the little things like getting a cold glass of water whenever you desire it or not having to wait in line for the shower, or just having some privacy. I relished in this freedom for the first couple of days, and then I had to get back to therapy for my knee. It was time to move onward and upward and once again make a life for myself.

Physiotherapy sessions were scheduled twice a week within a week of returning home. I knew that I would make better progress with Julie working with me one on one. I did or attempted to do everything Julie asked of me. Some tasks were awkward, other tasks were very painful to perform but I was relentless, I was not going to let anything hold me back now.

When I was at the rehab hospital, I was fitted for a special brace that would help with my foot drop, and my walking gait. Making this brace involved casting my foot and leg, as the brace would extend up the back of my leg, almost to my knee, then attach at the front of my leg with Velcro straps. The brace was made in two parts, the foot part which was then hinged to the leg part. The cost of this brace was about $1600.00. When I received the brace I had much difficulty putting it on by myself. I had trouble fitting my foot while in the brace, into my shoe and when I finally got the shoe on it felt a little snug. It was obvious that I would have to buy new walking shoes either one half or one full size larger.

The brace definitely played a role in improving my walking gait and also the foot drop. However, it was not without its faults. When I walked it made a clicking sound, the plastic that extended up the back of my leg got quite warm and would make my leg perspire, and there was an area at my ankle bone that became a pressure point from the brace rubbing in that spot. I was able to pad this area with foam, which helped to alleviate some of the pressure that had previously been a problem.

I wore this brace for many months but found it to be

quite cumbersome and gradually weaned myself off of it.

As after previous surgeries, my mother-in-law came and stayed with Randy and I for two weeks when I returned from the hospital. Having her in the house to help with various aspects of daily living was a Godsend. She was able to help get meals prepared, clean up after meals, assist with laundry, answer the phone and take me to physio appointments. The best part was having someone else in the house for company and security. In the afternoons we would often chat over a cup of tea, discussing anything and everything. My mother-in-law and I also shared the fact that we both enjoyed knitting. She and I bought various colours of funky yarn and knit many scarves each. I would later donate these scarves at Christmas to needy mothers and teenage girls, as well as giving them to friends and family members. I considered knitting to be a form of therapy for my right hand so there was a benefit to me as well.

After my mother-in-law returned to her home, my house once again became very quiet and I had more time on my hands. I used this time to exercise my knee more. I worked on both extension and flexion of my right knee, but the knee still remained stiff.

H. Anne Sinotte

In my physio sessions, Julie worked tirelessly with me to increase the degree of extension and flexion. I made sure I took analgesics prior to physio sessions, because having less pain facilitated a more productive workout. There were days when Julie was stretching my leg that I cringed from the pain, but I didn't want her to stop because this was all for my benefit.

Julie also put much effort into trying to reduce the tension in my right great toe, which was a result of the drop foot as well as nerve damage. This toe had now become very arthritic. Sometimes when Julie was manipulating this toe I could feel and hear scar tissue being broken up, and I did get some pain relief when this occurred.

On physio days I always went early so that I could exercise using some of the equipment. One of my favourite pieces of equipment was the recumbent bike. I would get on the bike and pedal frontward's as far as my degree of bend would allow, and then pedal backwards in the same manner. I was determined that I would someday have enough degree of bend to be able to complete the pedal rotation both frontward's and backwards. To my delight, one day months later I was able to complete the pedal rotation in the backwards mode. Within a

H. Anne Sinotte

couple of weeks I could do this pedalling frontward's, even though I was hiking my hip a little in the process. My next feat was to do this without involving my hip, and with persistence I won this battle as well. I was so proud because it meant I was increasing the degree of flexion at my knee.

Shortly after my return from hospital in March 2008, I received papers from our automobile insurance company to pursue investigations as to whether or not my case should be given a catastrophic designation. This is something that is not done until two years after an accident, with specific criteria to be met before application for catastrophic would even be considered. The main difference with this status is that the insurance coverage amount would increase significantly along with the years of coverage.

Even though it was my choice to have the application completed by the appropriate source, to pursue the avenue of catastrophic, I now wished it wasn't pending. The package I received from the insurance company was large, well organized and a little intimidating. The package contained all the appointment dates and times with each Health Professional, the education and credentials of each health professional, a map showing the location of the testing facility, the question to the medical examiner and the original application for Determination of Catastrophic Impairment.

There were appointments made for me for an entire week, sometimes with two appointments in one day. The final appointment was for one day the following week, making a total of five days of appointments and or testing. These appointments were scheduled with a neurologist, orthopaedic surgeon, occupational therapist, psychologist, psychological testing, chiropractor and ophthalmologists, all of whom I had never met before. The appointments were scheduled in a larger city within my geographical area. The insurance company would provide transportation if I so needed it.

Initially I remember thinking that this was an exhausting challenge for someone without physical or emotional concerns but for someone like myself with my numerous complaints, doing all of this in one week, plus the travel time involved, was a nightmare.

April 2008 arrived and I continued having physiotherapy. I could see some improvement but my right knee was still stiff and painful. I did exercises and worked my knee every chance I got but it remained tight.

On one of my follow-up appointments in April in Toronto with the orthopaedic surgeon, he too thought that the knee joint was tight, so he ordered the JAS splint system for my right knee for four months. This meant having to apply this splint three times a day for thirty minutes each time, the same as I had two years prior to my right ankle. Sometimes it felt like I never had any time just for me. It seemed that everything I did was medical related, but of course I would add this to my daily regime because it was all for my own good. I used the JAS splint from April to August 2008, and it did help to loosen my knee so that it would move more freely.

* * * * *

Mid April arrived and now it was time to attend all these appointments set up by the insurance company. I prepared any paperwork that I thought might be helpful to the various disciplines. Other than that I just had to be myself and let each person see my injuries and me exactly as presented...there was nothing to hide, everything was quite visible other than the emotional scars.

The first day of testing was with an Occupational Therapist for a duration of five hours. I arrived by taxi a short time before my appointment. I entered the building ambulating with my walker, announced myself at reception, and then took a seat as requested. A short while later, the O.T. came and got me and proceeded with her assessments. At first she took a history, concentrating in depth on the snowmobile accident. Sometimes the rehashing of the accident would make me very emotional, reducing me to tears, even though I have gone over the details of the accident numerous times. The O.T. put me through many assessments and I was happy when the five hours was up and I could go home. I only had to wait a few minutes for the taxi to arrive. When I got home fifty minutes later, I was exhausted. The first thing I did was lie on the sofa for a short rest before dinnertime.

The next day my appointment wasn't until noon and it was only for one hour so not such a heavy day. This appointment was with a chiropractor. He basically had me moving in various positions involving my back, legs, hands, neck and head. During these movements he took measurements of every joint being put through flexion and extension.

H. Anne Sinotte

It seemed like my body parts were twisted and turned into positions they never reached before. I was relieved when all the measurements were completed. In total the measurements took just over one hour to complete.

I had one day clear in the middle of the appointments that I did not have any testing to be done. I spent that day resting on the sofa, because I was so exhausted. Going back and forth and constantly being assessed was very tiresome.

The following day I had two assessment appointments, one first thing in the morning with an orthopaedic surgeon, then one immediately afterwards with a neurologist. Each of these appointments was to be one hour in duration.

Once again the structure of the appointments resembled the previous ones. I was asked to give a brief medical history then a more in-depth account of the accident, injuries sustained, treatments and surgeries done, and current concerns and outcomes.

I found the orthopaedic surgeon to be very thorough in his assessment and examination of the injuries sustained to my right hand, knee and tibia. He performed range of motion to the fingers of my right hand, right knee, right foot and toes and took measurements of the degree of flexion and extension in these joints. He questioned me about my level of pain and medications used for pain control. This doctor was pleasant throughout his examination and when finished assisted me in finding the room to be used for my next appointment.

There was no time between appointments to get my bearings. This appointment was with a neurologist for a neurological assessment. This involved many questions being asked of me as well as me providing a list of all my current complaints. The neurologist also tested all of my reflexes and had me perform different balancing and sensory tests. Before I knew it the hour set aside for this evaluation was up and it was time for me to go home.

The next day was Friday and I had to be at the testing centre for 8:30 a.m. This day was delegated as neuropsychological assessment day. The testing that was done was much the same as the testing I had done at the general hospital in 2007. This testing is quite in depth and can be very frustrating for the person being tested. After lunch I just wanted to take a nap, I was so tired, but instead I went for a short walk outside to clear my head and get some fresh air. Finally, at about 4:00 p.m., I told the tester that I had enough and wanted to go home. At this point I was in tears from being emotionally drained. The tester saw that I could go no further so we ended the session and she called a cab to take me home. Upon arriving home I had to lie down and rest. I couldn't physically or emotionally deal with anything more that day.

My final appointment for this testing was the following Thursday in Toronto, with the ophthalmologist. When I entered the room where he was I was not impressed. I found him to be a little too old, his hands shook and he did not appear to be as competent as I would have liked. At any rate this doctor completed his examination of my right eye and I left the clinic.

At this point in time all the testing was completed for this Catastrophic Impairment Evaluation. I had done my part, now all the doctors and disciplines involved would have to complete their reports with their findings and have a case conference to reveal their decision.

Time passed and I put this evaluation out of my head. Sometime in early June 2008 I received a large envelope delivered by Purolator. Upon opening the envelope I discovered it was from my insurance company. This was a very large document, sixty-eight pages in total. A letter accompanied the document, stating that the Insurer's Examination shows that I suffered a catastrophic impairment under the Statutory Accident Benefit Schedule,

Wow, this was a huge victory for me. Now I could put this behind me and move forward. It felt weird being declared catastrophic, but I think this is justified by the severity of my injuries and all that I lost as a result of the accident. As a result of this decision, at least financially, I wouldn't have to worry about medical needs being covered.

H. Anne Sinotte

All you need is love. Love is all you need.
John Lennon

Chapter Fifteen
As Good As It Gets

This accident took its toll on me both physically and emotionally. In the beginning it was questionable whether I would survive the numerous injuries I sustained. Then when it appeared that I was out of the woods, critically speaking, the tides changed to whether or not I would ever walk again or if in fact my right leg might have to be amputated. My right hand didn't work the way it did prior to the accident...my grip was gone and weight bearing status was greatly reduced. I suffered on-going headaches probably because of the head injury or maybe as a result of the frightening nightmares or "flashbacks" of the accident. Initially, my speech and thinking process was affected increasing my level of frustration as I tried desperately to find the words I was searching for, or to communicate a thought in a manner that would be understood.

At first much of what I said and did was

choreographed by all the medication I was receiving, especially the analgesics which put me in an entirely different world. It didn't matter if it was day or night; it was all the same to me. Slowly I was weaned off or at least cut back in the amount of analgesic I was taking. Of course I then saw things more clearly but this also brought the reality of the situation to the forefront. This created a whole new problem, depression and posttraumatic stress disorder. Upon learning of the reality of what happened to me I wished that I had died in the accident. I couldn't imagine my life as a disabled person in a wheelchair and even worse I didn't want to be a burden to my husband or have him resent me because of all the care I would need.

On one particular visit while I was still in hospital I asked Randy to leave me. I explained my reason for this and told him that he should get on with his life and seek out whatever it took to bring happiness back to him. I told him that I would be okay, that I no longer required a large living space, so I could search for a small ground floor, handicap accessible place to live. I even told him that I loved him enough to set him free. Randy was tremendously hurt by my suggestions and has remained by my side through the good and the bad. I am a very lucky person to have been blessed with such a

H. Anne Sinotte

dedicated, unselfish, caring partner...my soul mate.

Perhaps facing reality is what motivated me to be strong and gave me the courage and determination to do everything humanly possible to improve my physical outcome. I stopped feeling sorry for myself and instead put everything I had in me, into getting better. I pushed myself in physiotherapy until my body ached and could take no more. This paid off as I developed a strong upper body as well as toning and strengthening my left lower body. These areas would compensate for the lack of movement and strength on the right side of my body. In occupational therapy where concentrated flexion and extension range of motion exercises were performed on my right hand, I allowed the aide to work on my hand until I literally cried out in pain, because I could not endure any more.

This activity occurred every day and continued until I left the rehab hospital and even though I was in a wheelchair I also learned how to use a walker and was competent doing so for short distances.

Nothing changed much when I came home from hospital, except that I was working one on one with a physio and occupational therapist. The treatments were intensive and focused on particular areas such as extension of my knee, ankle therapy, passive exercises to loosen the tightness in my great toe and exercises targeting my foot drop. The occupational therapist continued with many different treatments to strengthen and improve function in my hand. I was able to look forward to these sessions because the pain factor was removed.

I continued with occupational therapy for a few months, and then my physiotherapist took over the hand therapy. She was aware of the treatment I needed to the hand and thought if she took it over, it would decrease the number of appointments I would have to attend. This plan worked well and Julie made great strides in improving the range of motion to my baby finger.

* * * * *

It is now five years later and I have realized that my progress and improvement is as good as it gets. I have progressed from the bed, to a wheelchair, to a standard walker, to a wheeled rolator walker, to walking with two canes, to walking with one cane. I am proud of myself for having the perseverance to reach this outcome.

My hand has improved to the point that I have a

H. Anne Sinotte

semi-grip. Things aren't perfect and there are definitely limitations, but at least I can use my hand again and I have increased strength in my hand.

The foot drop I experience is directly related to the loss of perineal nerve function. It is obvious that after all these years this nerve will never regenerate to the extent that the foot drop will go away. To compensate for this problem I have had lifts put on the right foot of several of my most commonly worn shoes. This also helps to improve my walking gait.

My vision has been stable; I am followed every six months by the ophthalmologist for visual field tests and measuring of the pressure in my eyes. Continued elevated pressure could indicate the onset of glaucoma. My eyes become more tearful and eyestrain occurs more easily, so I rest my eyes at those times.

One of the biggest changes I've had to make since the accident was a lifestyle change. Living in northern Ontario, we experience cold, snowy winters. The first couple of winters after the accident were rough and difficult for me to get around. When there was snow or ice on the ground, I lost all confidence and was deathly afraid of falling. I would not go outdoors unless I had a medical appointment. As a result I was cooped up for most of the winter, going nowhere and seeing no one. Randy and I decided that this was no way to live.

In January 2009 we rented a condo in Florida for three months. What a difference this made for both of us and especially to our quality of life. For me it meant I could get outdoors every day and walk around the small community where we were staying, without worrying about weather conditions, which would affect my footing. We loved this area of Florida so much with the unique style of condos overlooking the golf course. Actually the condos were more like little "cottages".

Towards the end of our time in March 2009, an opportunity presented itself mad Randy and I purchased a condo in this same community. We were thrilled with our purchase...the condo was in pristine condition but needed our personal touch to make it home. Our little cottage is located on a golf course overlooking the eighteenth hole with a fabulous panoramic view of the eighteenth fairway...just incredible!

We decided that since we now owned property in Florida, we would spend five to six months there every year. We would likely leave for Florida towards the end of October and return to Canada around the middle of April, each year. Now Randy and I had something to look forward to, we could make this little "cottage" our winter home.

> A real friend is one who walks in when the rest of the world walks out.
> *Walter Winchell*

<u>Chapter Sixteen</u>
<u>Reflections...All That I Have Lost</u>

This accident was certainly a life-altering experience, especially for someone like myself. Prior to the accident I could have been compared to the Energizer Bunny. I kept going and going and going. Having this type of disposition made adjusting to this new lifestyle very difficult and overwhelming to say the least.

Five months of my life was spent in hospital. I suffered a disconnection from what was happening outside of the hospital walls, including being apart from my family, friends, coworkers and the world in general. I often felt so isolated even when people visited me, because I didn't know what to talk about because I didn't know what was happening outside of my little world. On the receiving end, it sometimes felt like I was being humoured, partly in fact because people didn't know what to say to me. I remember thinking how simple I felt and did not know where I fit in anymore...a misfit, a cast away...

These feelings became more pronounced as I started to get better, I could see the physical changes in myself and the accompanying limitations. These limitations would change my life forever.

The biggest and most frustrating loss was my independence; I required assistance with so many aspects of activities of daily living such as; getting washed, dressed, showered, preparing meals and ambulation. These are things that most of us take for granted as I previously had done. Now these activities seemed like huge chores because I had to depend on someone to help me, at their convenience, which was not necessarily when, I needed the help. I needed someone to be with me at all times, I couldn't be left alone...it was unsafe for me. I could fall when transferring position or require assistance with toileting needs. The list goes on and on. The worst part was that I felt I was about twenty-five years older than I was. The care I was receiving was the same care I gave my patients... it was sort of ironic to have the tables turned.

Losing body function became such a challenge. At

H. Anne Sinotte

first it was because my right leg just didn't work. Getting myself from point A to B was most difficult. Couple that; with my dominant right hand that also didn't work and this was a total fiasco. Gripping the walker was a huge problem. My hand would ache and become cramped. I had to pad the grips on the walker so that I could use it properly.

As time passed and I had my right knee replaced, I experienced a whole other set of concerns. Bending was very painful and I couldn't kneel down as this could cause damage to the replaced knee. If I was on the floor I would have to get up in the same manner as a toddler, planting my feet on the floor and pushing my rear end up in the air in order to straighten up...not very becoming!

In light of these changes, I lost my self-esteem and how I viewed my body image. At times I felt like a freak in a sideshow. I saw how people viewed me, and then whispered comments to each other. I was so affected that I found myself wanting to explain why I looked this way or why I walked the way I did. It was almost easier when I was in a wheelchair because all people saw was the wheelchair and not the person in the wheelchair. Over time I got used to the looks and the whispers and learned to ignore it all by realizing that the

H. Anne Sinotte

people who did this didn't know any better.

Sometimes it is still difficult to look at myself, my right leg is grossly scarred from the numerous surgeries I have had and my right hand is a little deformed looking because of the constant bend in my baby finger, yet the baby finger tends to stick out causing it to get caught on things all the time.

After over five years I have come to accept the fact that it is what it is and I cannot change what has happened and the damage that has been done. My self-esteem will never be the same as prior to the accident and this is just something I have to get accustomed to and get on with life.

A huge loss was not being able to drive my car. I didn't have my driver's licence suspended or taken away. I made the choice not to drive because at first I was incapable and later on it did not feel safe for me to get behind the wheel. I waited until after the knee replacement in 2008. Several months later I asked the surgeon for his opinion regarding my driving again. He related that I should first practice driving in a secluded area to get my bearings again. If I was comfortable with my driving then I could attempt venturing out in a little more traffic as long as I had someone else in the car with me for support. He also stated that if driving was too overwhelming I should perhaps take a few re-training lessons.

My biggest concern was the use of my right leg on the gas and brake pedals. Would I be able to move my leg quick enough to react to sudden braking? I practised this with Randy and he commented that my reflexes were much sharper than he expected. I drove a few times with Randy in the car but then had the confidence to set out on my own. I found myself being more cautious than I used to be and stuck pretty closely to all speed limits. I didn't make risky turns that I previously would have as my driving became more defensive.

I was so thrilled being able to drive again, not having to depend on someone else to chauffeur me around. I was also proud of myself; that two and a half years after the accident I made such strides to be able to get behind the wheel of a car again. To have my independence boosted this way was such a feat.

One of the greatest challenges of loss was my career. For almost twenty years I had specialized in gerontology. Working with the elderly was my passion and niche. I advocated for these people who were either incapable or too frail to advocate for themselves. I enjoyed going to work and being with these individuals who played a huge role in moulding our country. I learned a great deal from the elderly and most people would if they would just take the time to listen to them.

Since graduating from nursing school in 1973, being a caregiver was what I did and I did it well. Making a difference in someone's life could be life changing for that individual and rewarding to me. What would I do with the energy and passion I poured into my career?

It became obvious to me that I would not be able to return to nursing in the capacity I had loved...the hands on aspect. I may have been able to find work in an administrative level but did not want to do management work anymore. I knew my body couldn't cope with the physical demands of working on a nursing unit anymore, so I made the decision to resign from the part-time position I currently held. The decision to resign was extremely difficult to make, but if I couldn't give 120% of myself to the job as I had in the past, then I wouldn't compromise the integrity, compassion and dedication that was synonymous with the nurse I was throughout my career. Leaving nursing was one of the most upsetting, heart-wrenching things I have ever had to do in my life.

H. Anne Sinotte

A true friend is someone who is there for you when they're supposed to be somewhere else.
Linda MacFarlane

Chapter Seventeen
Count My Blessings

Reflecting back on what could have been, I count my blessings for all that I have and all that I am. I thank the good Lord for saving my life and for giving me strength and courage to be where I am today. I may not be perfect, but I still have two legs, two arms and a brain that functions. Every part of me now functions at a much slower pace but I am still able to function and be a part of society.

I know that I can no longer do in one day what I did before but that is okay, I've learned my limitations and accepted that as my new "normal".

One of my favourite prayers that I have frequently referred to, to guide me through the last twenty-nine years of my life, is The Serenity Prayer. I recited this prayer numerous times since the accident and I was always left with a peaceful calm afterwards.

H. Anne Sinotte

*God grant me the **serenity** to accept the things I cannot change,*
*The **courage** to change the things I can, and*
*The **wisdom** to know the difference.*

I used these principles to help me move forward in a realistic and healthy manner.

I **could not change** the fact that the accident happened and I sustained multiple traumas to various parts of my head and body. I **could change** my attitude regarding recovery and rehabilitation, which could directly affect the outcomes of improvement. The **difference** is I had to learn that I could overcome this tragedy if I had faith in myself, by converting my energy into strength and courage to meet the demands of recovery.

When I felt that I was at the end of my rope, I would repeat this prayer over and over until the appropriate answer or action became clear to me.

Even though becoming disabled took time to adjust to and accept, I count my blessings that I wasn't born with these physical handicaps. As I discussed earlier on in this book, the challenges faced by the disabled sometimes seem insurmountable and although public awareness has definitely been heightened, there is still a long way to go to foster understanding and create a more seamless society.

My greatest blessings would have to be my husband Randy and sons Kevin and Brad. Randy was by my side almost daily. He would not be daunted by the situation or possible outcomes. He held tight to his vision that I would get better and be able to lead a productive life once again. Randy refused to let his hopes wane where I was concerned. I drew on Randy's strength and his faith in me to improve. Randy was my rock, my safe harbour if you will that I could go to at all times. I cannot imagine what it would have been like going through this ordeal without him...he is my strongest weakness.

Kevin and Brad came to visit when they could because they both had jobs to attend. Kevin lived in Whitby and Brad lived in St. Catharine's, so they were both out of town. At first it was devastating for them to see me their mother all battered and broken and so close to death, but with time they were able to see beyond all that and assist me with ambulation and some of my rehab exercises. Both of my sons are very caring individuals who would offer help to anyone in need. I am proud of both of them and I feel so fortunate to have them in my life.

H. Anne Sinotte

Family and friends played a major role in getting me through this most trying of times. My three brothers and their wives and kids came to visit on a regular basis. They encouraged me to fight for my life and they supported me through the many challenges that occurred, especially in the first year after the accident.

This tragedy took its toll on my dad, as he appeared to be going through a rapid decline in his health. Thank goodness dad lived with my brother Mark, so at least Mark could keep an eye on him...another blessing to add to my count.

My friends were remarkable they were lifesavers. I had many, many friends visit me in the five months I was in hospital and I am grateful to each of them for their support, prayers and love. Out of the multitude of friends three stand out as true angels, angels without wings...Pat, Lynn and Jackie. These three went above and beyond to show me how much they cared and wanted to be there for me. Their frequent visits, their smiles, their gentle touch, their interest in being involved with my care and recovery were overwhelming. They were awesome. There were times that I wondered if Pat ever left my side, it seemed like she was always there...for the good as well as the not so good. I am in awe of my friends and could never give back to them all they have given to me. Yes my friends are angels without wings and I count my blessings everyday that they are a part of my life.

These blessings made me realize what was important and my way of giving back was to get better, to fight with all my strength and being, to be in a better place with each one.

H. Anne Sinotte

> For daily need, there is daily grace; for sudden need, sudden grace; and for overwhelming need, overwhelming grace.
>
> *John Blanchard*

Chapter Eighteen
A New Day

Here it is five years since my accident and the changes that have occurred are phenomenal. I have been through a horrible battle and have emerged a survivor.

I am a better person and a stronger person as a result of the trials and challenges I have faced. I know exactly where I have been and how hard I fought to rise above the difficulties and countless hurdles along the way. This experience has been a humbling one, leaving me with renewed hope for the future and enhanced insight of the person I have been inspired to be.

Writing this book has been a tremendous source of accomplishment for me. It has challenged me to exercise my mind by making me think carefully about the facts encompassing this incident. It has helped me to strengthen my language and spelling

H. Anne Sinotte

skills. Most importantly, it has helped me to put this ordeal in prospective.

This is a new day, a new life and there will be new adventures for me to explore.

I give thanks to my Heavenly Father for embracing me during this time of need.

*****

I had intended on ending this book at this point, but as life would have it, another huge challenge came along.

H. Anne Sinotte

H. Anne Sinotte

Part Two

H. Anne Sinotte

Where there is great love, there are always miracles.
Willa Cather

Chapter Nineteen
...Five years later, January 11, 2011

January 11, 2011 almost five years from the day of my snowmobile accident, I am about as good as I will get physically and am trying to make a life for myself in this new "normal."

Unfortunately, my plans would have to be put on hold for a little longer. For the past several weeks I had been experiencing pain in my left flank area and above my left kidney, I used my nursing knowledge to rule out possible reasons for the pain, but the pain just wouldn't go away. Randy and I were wintering at our cottage in Florida and as Canadians we had a lot of red tape to go through for insurance purposes in order to seek medical attention. I telephoned the insurance company we were using to inquire about the protocol for getting medical care. After speaking to the insurance representative, I was advised to go to a particular hospital within our geographical area. The insurance company had a contract with this particular hospital for out of country claims.

Randy and I had a late breakfast then headed to the designated emergency department. While Randy parked our vehicle, I registered then took a seat in the almost full waiting room.

It was quite some time until the nurse called me into a room at which time she assessed me for the sole purpose of triaging. She checked my vital signs, gave me a urine specimen container to fill and showed me where to put it when I was finished. She then escorted me back to the waiting room.

I developed a troublesome cough within the previous 24 hours, so I donned a mask for infection control purposes.

Finally just before 3:00 p.m. I was taken in to a cubicle in the emergency room. This is when everything started to happen very quickly.

The ER doctor came in and took a medical history, then asked about the symptomatology of my current complaint. I explained that the pain felt like it originated just under the left rib cage, radiated to my left flank then around to my back over my left kidney. I explained that it was a nagging pain that would not go away. I had recently lost about 15 pounds and also found that I became tired out rather quickly.

After obtaining the info the doctor did a physical exam concentrating on the area of discomfort. He then ordered blood work, an EKG, chest x-ray and a CT scan without contrast of my chest, abdomen and pelvis. Within minutes an IV was started, blood was drawn, cardiogram and chest x-ray were all completed. I barely returned from x-ray when someone came to escort me to have the CT scan done.

Once back in my cubicle it was just a matter of minutes before the doctor returned. Little did I know that my life was once again going to take a major shift?

The doctor tried to deliver the news as gently as possible. He started by saying that the good news was that I didn't have diverticulitis, diverticulosis or pneumonia. He took a deep breath then continued by saying, "the CT scan indicated that I had a large mass above my left kidney." I felt my lower lip start to quiver. He then added, "There were also lymph nodes seen in your chest." This is when I started to lose it because a mass and lymph nodes equal metastatic cancer. "I'm sorry to be the one to give you this news," he said.

The doctor went on to say that I should be admitted to hospital for further testing, including another CT scan but this time with contrast (contrast helps to illuminate the organs more clearly) to confirm this diagnosis. He then left Randy and I alone to digest what we had just heard.

After a few minutes Randy slipped out to phone the insurance company to get authorization for hospital admission, further testing, consultations and treatments. When Randy returned he informed me that authorization was granted. Little did he know that I could care less? All I could think of was this impending feeling of doom that my life was quickly going to come to an end.

This news today was far from good or encouraging. Another battle for me...how many more battles can I endure...life sure is not fair!

I decided to send Randy home to get something to eat. It was around 4:00 p.m. now and we hadn't eaten since around 10:00 a.m. While at the condo Randy could pick up a few things for me that I would need for my stay in the hospital.

While Randy was gone, my nurse kept bringing me the three contrast drinks I had to consume prior to my next CT scan. On one of his visits with me I complained that my cubicle was freezing and I couldn't stop shaking as a result. He agreed with me and found the hidden thermostat and cranked up the heat for me. I was so grateful when I started to regain warmth in my body again.

A short while later the doctor assigned to be my Primary Care physician arrived and introduced himself to me and explained his role in my case. He then proceeded to take a medical history after which he did a physical exam. He reiterated the findings of the CT scan and the diagnosis of metastatic cancer and then asked Randy and I if we had any questions. The primary care physician also informed us that he had requested a surgical consult as well as a medical oncologist consult. My head was swimming with questions but I decided to wait until the tests were in and consults were done.

It was about 6:15 p.m. when I was taken to have my second CT scan done. This scan would produce a better picture as the liquid contrast I drank would illuminate the tissues, while the IV contrast would make the organs more clear to see. I forgot how much the dye stung when it was going through the vein, perhaps because the site of injection was my hand. The other thing was the incredible feeling one had as the dye was dispersed, that it felt like you were peeing your pants, which you weren't, but I still had to check myself afterwards.

I was returned to the ER cubicle and it was only minutes later when the ER doctor came in to tell me that the scan I just had confirmed that I indeed had metastatic cancer, origin unknown.

* * * * *

At the change of shift, 7:00 p.m. my day nurse came in to say goodnight and he wished me well. Shortly after the night nurse came in, introduced herself to Randy and myself and offered empathy over my diagnosis. She then asked if I was hungry and offered to bring me a sandwich and a drink. She then extended the same offer to Randy. She left but returned promptly with the food and drinks for us. I know that Randy appreciated the food because he was not able to eat when he went home earlier, so it was no surprise to see his sandwich disappear so quickly.

H. Anne Sinotte

It was around 8:00 p.m. when I was wheeled to my room on the fifth floor. It was a semi-private and I had the window bed. The RN and aide were there to orientate me to my new surroundings. The RN took the usual history in order to develop my plan of care. The aide took my vital signs and assisted me with getting settled in. I was only in my new room about twenty minutes when the surgeon came to do his consultation. He again asked me a multitude of questions, examined me and informed me that he would be consulting with the primary care physician and oncologist for the appropriate treatment of my cancer. He asked if there were any questions then left shortly thereafter with the promise of seeing me tomorrow.

By this time I was so very tired that I just wanted to close my eyes and shut off the entire world. However, I could not stop coughing. This respiratory infection was wearing me down. It was a dry, tickle of a cough that proceeded to worsen as the day went along. I coughed so frequently and with such force that I thought I would be sick to my stomach.

Sleep was not to be had as the cough persisted all night. I got up and walked around, drank water, read a book but to no avail. Finally, exhausted as I

H. Anne Sinotte

was I just gave up and waited for morning to arrive.

Once the day nurse came on duty, I asked her if she could contact the primary care physician to obtain an order for a cough suppressant for me. I was booked for a biopsy later in the day and I had fears of hacking away with a needle stuck in me.

The nurse did get some cough syrup ordered for me and I was given a dose prior to going down for the biopsy.

It was about 2:45 p.m. when an attendant came with a wheelchair to take me to Nuclear Medicine for the biopsy. Randy escorted me to Nuclear Medicine but made himself scarce for the actual procedure. Once inside the room both the technician and the doctor explained the procedure to me and had me sign consent. I became more and more anxious as the procedure was being done only with local anaesthetic...I would be awake throughout the procedure.

The doctor was terrific and explained that if I had any discomfort during the procedure to speak out and he would inject more xylocaine to make me more comfortable. The technician started to prep me. She was applying Betadine to my right pelvic area. I stopped her stating that all cancer areas were on the left side of my body. She reviewed her paperwork and read to me the area to be biopsied was a chain of lymph nodes in the right pelvic area. I felt panicky because now I knew that the cancer had spread to yet another site. My prognosis was becoming bleaker by the minute. I had to calm myself in order to safely get through this procedure. The technician finished prepping me then let the doctor know everything was ready to go.

The doctor entered the room and I took a deep breath because it was now "show" time. I felt a pinch as he inserted a needle with xylocaine into my right pelvic area and I did flinch as he went deeper to anaesthetize the lower tissue. He then inserted the biopsy needle into the lymph node. Once he was in position he then had the technician start the CT scan that moved me into the machine. He then used the CT pictures as a guide for needle placement in securing the biopsy. Following this I was then brought back out of the scanner to have the next biopsy taken, but this time with deeper penetration. I gasped as I could feel the needle; so more xylocaine was added enabling the doctor to carry on. This sequence of events was repeated until all specimens were collected.

H. Anne Sinotte

Once finished, the doctor showed me the jar containing the specimens. They looked like little brown worms. He congratulated me on being a good patient, and then I had an acute coughing spell, which at least held off during the procedure. The technician cleaned me up and placed a band-aid over the biopsy site. I was then placed on a stretcher and taken back up to my room.

I was relieved to have the biopsy done; now all I wanted was to sleep. The past two days had been such an emotional whirlwind for Randy and me, with all the testing, going back and forth, repeating accounts of my current illness to doctors and other medical personnel, hearing my diagnosis and trying to understand it and what it meant for my future.

The biopsy had to be sent to An Arbour Michigan to isolate the type of cancer cell and the primary source.

I spent two more days in hospital. Surgery was ruled out due to the spread of cancer. Radiation was also ruled out for the same reason. It was concluded that chemotherapy would be my best option. The insurance company was now pushing to get me back to Canada for treatment. It would not be approved for me to have treatment in the United

States.

On the second night in hospital Randy and I went to the chapel to pray, apparently Randy had gone to the chapel the previous evening as well. I said a silent prayer, signed the guest book then returned to my room.

I was discharged from hospital on Friday evening January 14th. I was totally impressed with the care I was given by doctors, nurses and other medical staff. The speed in which tests were done and a diagnosis made was phenomenal. If I were at home in Canada, a diagnosis would not have been obtained so quickly. I thanked everyone involved in my case for everything they did for me and we left the hospital. I was given instructions to phone the oncologist the following week to obtain the results of my biopsy.

While I was in the hospital, Randy did his best to get the ball rolling in Canada for my treatment. He contacted my family doctor and faxed my medical records from Florida to her. Randy explained to my doctor's receptionist that I would need a referral to a medical oncologist. He also told her that the Florida doctors indicated that treatment should be started immediately. Little did I know that all

Randy's good intentions would be ignored?

It felt good to get back home to our little cottage. I found that I was so emotional so I had to keep myself busy. I spent the weekend packing up things that needed to go back to Canada and put everything in the spare bedroom. I also prepared the cottage as best as I could for closing. The insurance company was flying us home to Canada on Tuesday, January 18th. Randy would have to fly back down in a few weeks to close the cottage and bring our vehicle home. What a crazy time this was!

All of our friends and neighbours in Florida came to say goodbye and wish us well on the Sunday and Monday before our flight on Tuesday. It was so good to be surrounded by such caring people, but it was also very emotional. The tears never stopped flowing for those days. I was truly blessed to have these people in my life, praying for me and supporting me completely.

H. Anne Sinotte

> *Hope*
> *Is the thing with feathers that perches in the soul*
> *and sings the tune without words and never stops ~*
> *at all.*
> *Emily Dickenson*

Chapter Twenty
Reflecting Back to 1982

On the flight home to Canada, I couldn't help reflecting back to almost 29 years earlier. A rush of distant memories flooded my brain, remembering those life altering days starting October 1982 when I was diagnosed with breast cancer.

I was a young wife, thirty years of age with a wonderful husband and two little boys, Kevin four years old and Bradley just barely two years old, when I received this blood curdling diagnoses. My life of adversity did not start at age 54 in a snow mobile accident but instead has been on-going since age 30.

Where do I begin, as always with the discovery that

I indeed had a potentially serious concern...I found a lump in my breast? The lump was hard, immovable and painless, but very real. My first reaction was that this could not be happening to me, as I was too young for breast cancer.

I immediately set up an appointment with my family doctor to have this thing checked. During that visit the doctor did not indicate anything to me but instead scheduled me for a mammogram as well as an appointment with a surgeon for follow-up and a second opinion.

A couple of days later, I had my very first mammogram. What a treat that was, the pulling, squeezing and positioning were so uncomfortable. As the machine compressed each breast it felt like my breasts were being transformed into pancakes. This was one of the least dignifying tests I have ever experienced, but it was over thankfully and it was back to the waiting game.

The day before my appointment with the surgeon, Wendy my friend who was also my family physician's nurse, telephoned me with the results of my mammogram...it indicated that I had fibrocystic disease. Cysts... I could deal with that diagnosis.

H. Anne Sinotte

I was feeling somewhat more at ease the following day when I ventured to the surgeon's office. This was one of the same surgeons I worked with at the hospital, so it was different seeing him in this capacity. Once in the examining room I tried to relax as the doctor examined my breasts. He palpated the lump and attempted to move it but it did not move. He inquired as to whether I had pain in the area and I answered negatively. He then asked my permission to perform a needle aspiration of the lump, which I agreed to. He prepped the area, and then injected some local anaesthetic. The doctor then injected a long needle into the breast lump. Once in place I watched as he pulled back on the syringe to aspirate, there was no fluid entering the syringe. Right then I knew that this was not a cyst. When the surgeon proceeded to speak to me I noted the urgency in his voice and words. He stated he wanted me in the hospital as soon as possible to have a biopsy done. A "quick" section of the lump would be biopsied, and then sent to pathology to determine whether it was malignant or benign. The results would be reported back to the surgeon while I was still on the operating room table. My options would be to have a lumpectomy done, or have a radical mastectomy done or be closed up with no treatment at that time. This decision would have to be made prior to surgery with a consent signed indicating my choice.

My mind was frantic trying to absorb everything I was hearing. What choice did I really have? Lumpectomies in Canada in 1982 were not that successful, so I ruled out that option. To open me up, remove some tissue and close me again, was not practical, leaving me with the only logical choice and that was to have a mastectomy, should the lump be malignant. I made this decision based on the fact that my two boys were only four and two years old and they deserved to have their mom around for as long as possible.

At the end of my appointment, arrangements were made for me to enter the hospital on Monday and the surgery would be done on the Tuesday. I didn't have much time to prepare as it was already Thursday, basically three days to get my house in order, tell my mom who was unaware of any of this yet and my two neighbours who were good enough to look after my boys while I attended these appointments. Randy and I would have to make arrangements for the boys while I was in the hospital. Likely my mom would volunteer to keep the boys until I was well enough to take over.

The days at home slipped by so quickly, I kept

myself very busy to avoid thinking about what lay ahead. Before I knew it, it was time to go to the hospital. We took the kids to my parent's house and while there mom asked for my permission to share this concern with my three brothers. I hesitated at first, but then agreed that she could call them. At least if they knew before hand what was happening, it wouldn't be such a shock if the outcome of the biopsy did not go in my favour. It was so difficult saying goodbye to my babies. They were both too young to understand what was happening. I thanked God for my mom and dad and I knew the boys were in good hands.

* * * * *

I didn't sleep well the night before surgery...I just couldn't shut off my brain from the thoughts and scenarios that were flashing through my mind. Eventually, I gave up trying to sleep and the nurse insisted that I take a sleeping pill, which did lull me to sleep.

The morning of surgery was busy with all the prep work, starting an IV and so on. When I was in the bathroom, I did take the time to have one last look at myself naked. I touched my breast in such a way that it looked like I was saying goodbye to it. Tears

H. Anne Sinotte

rolled down my face as the reality of what might happen suffocated me. I had to calm down; I couldn't go into surgery being so upset.

A short time later Randy arrived and we sat together and conversed until the orderlies came to take me to the operating room. This was around 12:30 p.m. I said goodbye to Randy but by this time I was flying high from the pre-operative sedation the nurse injected about fifteen minutes earlier. I think I told him that I was going on vacation.

Once in the operating room, my only memories were briefly talking to the surgeon, moving from the stretcher to the OR table and after the anaesthetic was injected into my IV I had to count backwards from 100. I don't know if I made it to 98!

My next memory was waking up for a brief moment in the recovery room. My right hand immediately went to my left breast but there was so much padding and bandaging there that I couldn't determine what was done in surgery. I heard myself ask the nurse, "Did Dr. M... remove my breast?" Before the nurse could answer me I fell back asleep.

It was several hours later when I again awakened for a brief time from the effects of anaesthesia. This time when I opened my eyes, I saw Randy, my mom and my older brother Steve, all standing over me around the bed. My vision was obscured; I couldn't move my left arm and I felt pain and pressure in my left side of my chest. It wasn't my heart but something different. I heard my mom saying, "She feels so cold when I touch her." I also heard sobbing in the background but could not distinguish where it was coming from.

After that I drifted back to sleep and didn't awaken again until sometime in the middle of the night. The night nurse was at my bedside attending to me and insisted in a kind manner that I get out of bed with assistance of course and be taken to the bathroom. The nurse tried everything to get me to pee but I just couldn't void and had no desire to do so. She told me that she would have to catheterize me because it was well over twelve hours since I last voided.

In the next few minutes the nurse returned to my bedside with all the equipment needed for this procedure. When she catheterized me my bladder had been full so she left the catheter in because I was obviously unable to go on my own. When this procedure was done I again slept.

H. Anne Sinotte

Later that morning when I awoke to face the day I realized from the pain I felt and the thickness and tightness of the bandages on my chest that my breast was gone. As I digested what happened to me I started to cry. I was only thirty years old and I had cancer and now only one breast. I continued in this manner not giving any thought to my three other roommates. The day shift nurse then came in, checked my vital signs and spoke to me in a rather gruff tone. Bedside nursing was certainly not her forte. She then proceeded to put a basin of water, soap and towels on my over bed table and as she was walking out of the room she told me to get washed. Before I could respond she was out of sight. This made me cry again and I was still crying when my surgeon entered the room and approached me. He asked me if I was upset because of the outcome of surgery. I told him that of course I was upset about that but that wasn't the reason for this outburst. I then explained to him what the nurse had done and added that I didn't know how I was going to wash myself when my left arm was paralyzed and my right hand had an IV with a fracture board stabilizing it. I only had the tips of my fingers exposed for any use. The doctor excused himself at that time but told me he would return. When he did return he informed me that the nurse would be in to wash me.

H. Anne Sinotte

The surgeon then proceeded to tell me all about the surgery, that in fact the biopsy tested positive for malignancy, therefore, the breast was removed. He explained that I lost a great deal of blood so was given a transfusion of two units of blood. He told me I had a hemovac drain in to remove excess fluid...this would be removed by him when there was no further drainage. He told me that further testing would be done on the tissue obtained from the biopsy. This testing would tell us what type of cancer cell I had and also if it was hormone dependant. If the latter were positive I would then be treated with medication that would induce early menopause. This was a lot of info to take in and think about. The surgeon then told me we would cross each bridge when and if needed but in the meantime he wanted me to rest and regain my strength. On that note he told me he would be back to see me the next day and then he exited.

When Randy came to visit that morning I updated him about everything and we shared a few tender moments together. Of course I wanted to know how the kids were doing and of course they were fine, they were with their Nana and Papa and probably being spoiled. Before Randy left the hospital he spoke to the authorities about having me

H. Anne Sinotte

transferred to a semi-private room for which I had insurance coverage. The main reason for this was to allow me some privacy to deal with this cancer diagnosis and everything associated with it. I was moved the following day.

Several days after surgery I received the results of the tissue pathology. The cell type was isolated as an adenocarcinoma of the breast. This particular cell was not hormone dependant; therefore, I wouldn't be put into early menopause.

It was felt that the cancer was contained with the removal of my breast, so as a result I would not require further treatment. This was one small blessing for me.

* * * * *

After I was in the hospital for about ten days my surgeon asked me if I would like to have a day pass to leave the hospital to be with my family...I was ecstatic and jumped at the opportunity. I was going to be with my kids, Randy, mom, dad and my youngest brother Mark. I was so excited, nervous but excited. On the day of my pass, the nurse assisted me in getting dressed. The clothes I had worn into the hospital were now hanging on me, from the weight I lost. I had lost and incredible amount of weight...somewhere in the neighbourhood of twenty pounds. Oh well I wasn't going to have this spoil my day.

The time spent at my parent's house was awesome. I had to be careful with Kev and Brad as they both wanted to be in my lap and be held by mommy. Randy would place them in my lap and they were told that they couldn't squeeze mommy because she had a BOBO. They were wonderful and I ached to hold them again.

We had a fantastic dinner and later that evening one of my aunts and uncle popped in at my parents for a visit. This particular aunt did not use any tact when she spoke. She asked me what my problem was. I decided that sooner or later everyone would have to know what was wrong with me, so I took a deep breath and told her, "I have breast cancer and I had my breast removed." Her next comment blew me away, she said, "well you might live long enough to see your boys grow up." Any mother hearing a comment like that would be dumbfounded and I was no different. To avoid any further dialogue with this Aunt I excused myself and left the room. My emotions were soaring as tears streamed down my face. What a cruel, inconsiderate comment to

H. Anne Sinotte

make, but in order to console myself I had to look at the source of the comment. I had to shake this off and the best way was to be with my two little boys. I gathered them up and we went into the spare bedroom and I read the boys a bedtime story. As was the usual practice one story led to a second one. How I missed these special moments with the kids.

Randy and I settled the boys into bed, thanked mom for a delicious meal, and kissed mom and dad goodbye, then Randy drove me back to the hospital. I was physically and emotionally spent but it was a good tired.

A day or so later the surgeon decided to remove my hemovac, as there was no further drainage. Prior to the procedure I was given an analgesic injection and then my hands and feet were restrained to the bed. The doctor cautioned me that this would be very uncomfortable for me. The drain was positioned in my upper chest in a semi-circle shape. As the drain was being pulled out the pain I felt was excruciating...one of the most agonizing pains I had endured in my thirty years. When it was over the relief I felt was manifested by weeping.

I believe it was two days later that I was discharged from the hospital. I spent a total of two and a half

H. Anne Sinotte

weeks in hospital. I wasn't to do any lifting, cleaning or heavy work when I went home. Although I was happy to be returning home, I was also concerned about the challenges I would have to face at home, especially since Randy's dad had just moved in with us and he wasn't exactly the most understanding man. He was actually quite sexist. Fortunately, for me Randy was going to be at home with me for the first couple of weeks. I would welcome all the help I could get.

* * * * *

When I was discharged from the hospital I stayed at my parent's home for a couple of weeks. Staying with my parents made the transition from hospital to home easier. While there the home care nurse visited daily to change my dressing and to remove my sutures. Mom and dad were great with the boys and with me. I was able to recuperate with the rest I needed.

The return to my home was extremely challenging, I had to modify routines and activities due to the residuals of surgery. I still couldn't lift my left arm much above waist level, my chest still hurt and I was generally weak. I had to have rest periods during the day, so when the boys napped, I also lay down in order to re-charge my body. I found it very strange not being able to pick up the boys, I always had to sit down and have someone place them on my lap. I could only manage light housekeeping chores and preparing the day's meals. Even with reduced activity I was still exhausted at night.

I was unable to drive the car because of the paralysis in my left arm, so Randy would have to take me grocery shopping on Saturdays. Occasionally, my dad would take me shopping during the week while mom watched the kids. Our young lives were turned upside down, making us feel a great deal older than we were.

Of course the most difficult adjustment was how I cared for the children. It broke my heart that I couldn't play with them in the same manner as I previously had and being so young they couldn't totally understand why things were so different. Somehow we all got through this trying time. What the boys lacked from me physically, I made up for it with the love and protectiveness I enveloped them in.

As a young thirty-year-old woman, body image played a huge role in how I perceived myself. I found it very difficult looking at myself in the mirror or undressing in front of my husband, even though he never seemed affected from the loss of my breast. Deep down, I felt like an incomplete woman. My posture changed...I found myself scrunching my shoulders forward so that my breasts were less obvious. A had a soft prosthesis to wear temporarily, but it did not give me the confidence I needed, especially when I was around other people. I started to become depressed about my missing breast, how I looked, so much so that it changed the level of intimacy between Randy and myself...I always felt inadequate. After a while that depression grew into bitterness. Why did this have to happen to me at such a young age? Why didn't it happen to a much older woman? I also became bitter with the society we live in where so much emphasis is put on the perfect female body. The ads on television, and in magazines for bras or other products involving half naked women did not help this cause. The increased level of nudity on the movie screens and in television programs really started getting to me. It is no wonder young girls are getting the wrong messages about their bodies and are therefore causing damage to themselves through anorexia or bulimia. I even had problems finding clothes that would fit me properly. I required clothes that would cover my surgical scars and not reveal the lack of breast tissue on one side

H. Anne Sinotte

of my chest. I could go on and on about the numerous challenges for someone who has lost their breast, but at the end of the day it isn't going to make a difference in the grand scheme of things.

After my incisions started to heal and my chest wasn't as sensitive or painful, I went to a mastectomy boutique to be properly fitted for a silicone prosthesis and also post-mastectomy bras and a bathing suit. The owner of the boutique was a phenomenally dynamic lady who also had breast cancer so she could relate with her clients in an empathetic manner. The service she provided was personalized for each individual. I left the boutique with increased self-esteem and confidence. All of a sudden the world didn't seem to be such a gloomy place. The owner of the boutique and myself went on to become friends and when she died several years later; I became friends with her daughter who so graciously continued the business her mother had proudly started.

* * * * *

I had researched breast reconstructive surgery, had appointments with various surgeons and had gone as far as being booked for surgery but something inside me would not let me follow through with the

H. Anne Sinotte

surgery. To present day I still have strong doubts about reconstructive surgery that is why I have not pursued it.

The daunting thing about cancer is once you have had it one always lives in fear of its return. In my case, return it did three years later.

*****

Once again I found the lump in the centre of my chest where my previous surgical scar ended. This time around the surgeon thought that perhaps the lump was scar tissue. I was booked for outpatient surgery in January 1986. A memorable day this would always be as it was also the tragic day that the Challenger Space Shuttle exploded in space.

After surgery the surgeon came to speak to Randy and myself. I knew as he approached us that the news he was about to deliver was not going to be good. He began to tell us that the tissue removed was once again cancerous. This time the cancer had spread to my breastbone. Randy immediately held my hand as the tears rolled down my face. Dr. M. relayed how sorry he was that this was once again happening to me. He also told me that he was referring me to a Toronto Cancer Hospital for further investigation and treatment.

Of course I felt deflated as this cancer continued to violate my body. Why was I being subjected to another life-threatening experience? So many unanswered questions were going through my head for which I would have to wait for the answers.

* * * * *

The day arrived for my appointment at the cancer hospital in Toronto. I was very nervous in anticipation of the outcome of this consultation. After many questions, discussions and review of my health history, the panel of physicians came to a decision regarding treatment. It was decided that chemotherapy would not be beneficial for me, but radiation would be the treatment of choice. I would require nine weeks of treatment, five days per week for a total of forty-five sessions. A bolus or concentrated treatment from the site of surgery to the breastbone would be included as part of this treatment.

I was taken to the radiation department and was given a small tour so I would have some idea of how the department operated before my first day of treatment. I was also taken into a room to be prepared for radiation...this is where I was tattooed for treatments. The tattoos were landmarks for the technicians to use when positioning my body for the treatments.

As the day went along, many of my questions were answered but other concerns surfaced. One such concern was how I would get to the Toronto hospital every day. There was no way that Randy could drive me because he had to go to work and I had no one else in a position that I could ask. This was a huge problem for me. When I mentioned this at the hospital, I was given a phone number that I could contact to make arrangements for transportation with the Cancer Volunteer drivers. This certainly was the answer to my problem and at least relieved the stress to that aspect of my latest dilemma.

It wasn't long until I developed a routine with going to Toronto daily for my radiation. The treatment time was quite short; each treatment took about forty-five seconds. More time was spent with the prep work prior to treatment. The volunteer drivers transported two other patients with me so we couldn't return home until treatments were completed on all three of us. The drive home was usually quieter than the drive to the hospital. This

H. Anne Sinotte

was generally as a result of being fatigued and in my case there was some nausea involved due to the location of my radiation.

During the course of my radiation treatments we were staying temporarily with my parents while our new home was being built. Sadly, mom was also undergoing radiation and chemotherapy treatments, so our lives were a rollercoaster ride with the emotions within my parents' home. When mom was not tied up in treatments and feeling okay, she would look after the boys if needed, but they were both in school for full days now and I was usually home from the hospital before they returned home at the end of the school day. Mom and I took turns preparing the dinner meal as neither one of us ever felt totally well. We were both always extremely tired and drained from all of the treatments. Somehow, though we made it through yet another trying ordeal.

* * * * *

Approximately ten weeks later I finished all my radiation treatments. In some respects it felt like ten weeks of my life were put on hold, as I was so tired the entire time I received treatments. My skin where treated became severely burned, almost raw, much worse than a bad sunburn. I had to be particular with clothing I wore, choosing only very soft, loose fitting tops. Showering was difficult because of the water pressure to my chest, so I kept my back to the flow of the water. Adjustments were made to compensate for the effects of the radiation.

One of the most difficult adjustments I had to make was my fear of the cancer returning. I hated the feeling of living in fear, so I had to change my way of thinking to become more positive. I reviewed the details of my cancer from the first time in 1982, to this current setback in 1986. I realized that I had done everything possible to get better and put this cancer into remission. Whatever happened from here on forward was out of my control. The situation is what it is and I would have to learn to live one day at a time and count my blessings for each day that I lived in good health. Also the hospital would be scheduling me for regular follow-up checks, so I now needed to have faith in the doctors and my future.

H. Anne Sinotte

> *In my friend, I find a second self.*
> Isabel Norton

Chapter Twenty-One
Current Day - January 18, 2011

I was brought back to reality by someone tapping me on the shoulder...it was the flight attendant inquiring about which entree I would like for dinner. She commented that I had drifted far, far away and in fact, I had. After giving my dinner choice to the flight attendant, I returned my thoughts to the present.

* * * * *

After arriving back home in Canada, I checked in with my doctor's office only to find out that no arrangements had been made yet for me to see a medical oncologist. Jane the doctor's receptionist stated that she couldn't refer me until the primary source of my cancer was known. This was frustrating me but I was too weak to argue with her. A day later I phoned the oncologist in Florida. He had the results of my biopsy. The primary source was the lung and the type of cancer was an adenocarcinoma. I thanked him and he wished me well.

I immediately phoned my family doctor's office with this information. A few days later Jane called me with an appointment at a major Toronto Cancer Hospital. She gave me the name of the oncologist I was being referred to and the date of the appointment was February 3, 2011 at 9:00 a.m.

Unfortunately, when I saw Dr. R.O. he stated that there was little he could do for me because he is a radiation oncologist and I needed a medical oncologist. This annoyed me because Jane was told this and chose to ignore the facts...more precious time wasted. Dr. R.O. observed that I was having a lot of pain above my left kidney and inquired what I was taking for the pain, which at the time was Advil. He ordered me stronger pain medication and told me he could radiate the mass above the kidney...this would shrink the tumour as well as reduce my pain. I agreed to this. Later that afternoon I was prepped for radiation...given tattoos and a CT scan, plus a mould was made for my arms to rest in when I actually had radiation. This was a Thursday and my radiation was going to commence the following Wednesday for five treatments, weekdays from Wednesday, February 9th to Tuesday, February 15th.

I also asked Dr. R.O. to refer me to a medical oncologist closer to my home in Barrie, Ontario. I thought that having chemotherapy treatments in Toronto was just too far to travel, especially if I felt at all sick afterwards...the doctor agreed with me.

The doctor also told me that my cancer was not curable..............

It was a long day at the hospital and we did not get home until about 6:00 p.m. Both Randy and I were exhausted when we got home and quite upset with the news we received. That night Randy admitted to me that he was scared of what the future held.

I took the stronger pain pills, Oxycodone, which was effective in controlling my pain. The following Wednesday, February 9th I started radiation treatments. All of my appointments were around 5 p.m. at the Toronto Hospital. Usually by this time of day I am very tired, but unfortunately, these were the only available times with such short notice. The set-up and positioning for radiation took the most time. The actual radiation took a couple of minutes, even though it seemed longer. The machine rotated around my body, sending beams of radiation from four different angles...quite amazing the way it all works.

That evening we had only been home for about five minutes when the nausea I was having came to a head causing me to vomit. Nausea became a part of my day. As a result I was eating very little and continued to lose weight. Every day when I left the hospital after radiation, I prayed that I would make it home without being sick to my stomach. I also kept a "puke" bucket in the car. I mentioned my nausea to one of the technicians and on the Friday she had the doctor write me a prescription for stronger anti-nausea medication. That Friday I was sick to my stomach again after I got home from the hospital.

I rested up as much as I could on the weekend. On Sunday, February 13th, Randy flew to Florida to close up our condo and drive our van back home. It was good that our son Brad was meeting him in Toronto, and then they would fly to Florida together. I was going to miss Randy but this had to be done.

I had my last two radiation treatments on Monday

February 14th and Tuesday, February 15th. Carolyn, my neighbour across the street drove me to both appointments. Again the nausea was so bad on the way home, but I made it and went to bed as soon as I got home.

Randy and Brad arrived back in Canada on Thursday, February 17th and I was grateful for their safe return.

While going through radiation treatments, I experienced great fatigue. When I wasn't travelling to Toronto or having the treatments, all I wanted to do was sleep or rest. My body felt drained all of the time. I had to psyche myself up in order to get anything done.

Nausea was the other demon I was fighting. It had escalated towards the end of January and continued during the course of my radiation treatments. Along with the nausea came a lack of appetite. I was barely eating enough to keep a bird alive and this manifested itself with ongoing weight loss. I was so afraid of eating certain foods because I never knew which foods would cause me to be sick to my stomach. Sometimes there was neither rhyme nor reason, it just happened. I did discover that the nausea started to subside within a couple weeks of the radiation treatments being completed and believe me I welcomed this change.

The machines used for radiation were not as large and bulky as the ones used twenty-five years ago. Once again the set-up took much longer that the treatment itself.

When I finished the radiation treatments I was aware that I had to rest my body in preparation for future cancer treatments, even though further treatment was yet to be determined.

H. Anne Sinotte

When we can share--that is poetry in the prose of life.
Sigmund Freud

Chapter Twenty-Two
Consultation with the Medical Oncologist

While Randy was in Florida, I received a phone call with a date and time to be seen by a Medical Oncologist for consultation purposes. I will refer to this doctor as Dr. M.O.

* * * * *

February 23, 2011, this was the day for my consultation appointment with Dr. M.O. This appointment ended up being about three hours long. I learned many things during this consultation.

I learned that my cancer was staged as a Stage 4 Lung Cancer...this is as bad as it gets...pretty upsetting for me!

I learned that the doctor would obtain my biopsy

done in Florida and send it off for testing for EGFR (Epidermal Growth Factor Receptor). If my cancer tested positive for this then a different treatment would be started which would still leave the option of chemotherapy available to me if this other therapy was not effective.

In the meantime, I was to have another CT scan that would encompass the brain, chest, abdomen and pelvis, a complete body bone scan and blood work. I was so impressed with the receptionist at this clinic as she was able to get all these tests scheduled for the same day.

A follow-up appointment was made for March 15th with Dr. M.O. I had had all the tests previously ordered done on March 3rd so the doctor would have the results available to him for this return appointment. When the doctor entered the examination room, he first greeted both Randy and I then proceeded to inform us of the results of the tests.

The first piece of information we received was that I tested negative for EGFR therefore, that treatment would not be available to me...Dr. M.O. informed me that my blood work was all within normal limits and my CT scan and bone scan did not reveal any further spread of cancer. He then reviewed possible options for treatment with me, including; chemotherapy, no treatment, or the possibility of taking part in a clinical trial. The latter did not appeal to me because I would have to go to Toronto for this and at the end of the day I wouldn't know if I was getting medication or a placebo. I also would not entertain the idea of no treatment; therefore, I opted for chemotherapy. This choice was made with the doctor's input guiding my decision.

* * * * *

I reported back to the hospital on April 4, 2011. On this visit I had a PICC line or central line inserted by the radiologist. I was somewhat apprehensive about this procedure because there is always fear of the unknown and fear of the invasiveness of having a catheter thread through a major vein. As it turned out, the procedure went very well and I tolerated it much better than I thought I would. This PICC line would be used for blood draws, for administering the chemo medications and also could be accessed for injecting the dye for CT scans. I also had blood drawn and saw the doctor as a pre-requisite to my first chemo session the next day. I learned what chemo drugs I would be receiving and was given information sheets on both the chemo drugs,

Cysplatin and Gemcitabine. I was also given a prescription to fill for several anti-nausea medications to be taken on chemo days prior to chemo, and also a couple of these medications had to be taken for a few days following chemo. I also received information sheets regarding the anti-nausea medications.

Following this appointment, Brad took Randy and me out to dinner as an early combined Mother's and Father's Day gift. It was a lovely dinner or as Brad called it my "last supper" because of course no one knew how I would tolerate the chemotherapy.

*****

When I first met Dr. M.O., I was surprised at his youthfulness in relation to his chosen field. He could have been my son with his age being what it was...I was later to learn that he was in his mid to late thirties. From the first encounter with Dr. M.O., I was impressed with his candor. He chose his words carefully to reduce the blinding sting of honesty, but remained straightforward and up front throughout our relationship. His approach was aggressive which suited me considering my cancer was incurable. Whatever could be done for me to increase my quality of life and life span was welcomed. I appreciated the way he shared his professional expertise with me in such an easy and caring manner. When he spoke to me he looked me straight in the eyes and when I questioned him on various concerns he would stop what he was doing, put his pen down and give me his undivided attention. These are all qualities that won my trust and allowed me to put my faith in this man, who was making important decisions about my life. Together he and I would fight this wretched disease.

H. Anne Sinotte

The miracle is this--the more we share, the more we have.
Leonard Nimoy

Chapter Twenty-Three
Chemotherapy

Chemotherapy can be a very debilitating experience. It is almost like an out of body sensation. You want to will your body to fight the fatigue and all the side effects of chemo and the feelings of generally being unwell, but you can't. One becomes frozen in time, where no changes can be made; the body is forced into a state of limbo where the cancer becomes all consuming. It is impossible to make plans or think of the future. The cancer monopolizes every fibre of one's being, every thought, every function, all of the time. The chemo fights the cancer but in the process also battles the body, weakening the mind, body and soul. Through all this devastation, one must remain positive holding on to any shred of hope that this enemy will retreat, if only for a little while.

Facing delays in treatment due to low blood counts are not just disappointing but also frustrating. Delays mean the passing of time, dragging out chemo sessions into weeks and months, very precious time needed to set one's affairs in order, be with family and friends, and doing things on one's "bucket" list.

* * * * *

My chemo treatments were set-up that I would receive chemo two weeks in a row, then have one week off, then start the cycle again. Each chemo session would last for five to five and one half hours if all went well, longer if it didn't. The two drugs I received were Cysplatin and Gemcitabine, both extremely potent and with a multitude of side effects. I was given a variety of drugs to counteract some of the side effects, primarily nausea and vomiting. These drugs included: Emend, which was very expensive (3 pills for $125.00), Decadron which is a steroid, Zofran and Stemetil. These anti-nausea medications were not without side effects either so many of the problems I experienced throughout this time was due to the anti-nausea medications. This was a very demanding schedule and I prayed that I would be able to handle it.

* * * * *

April 5, 2011, this was my first chemotherapy

treatment and I was anxious, nervous and quite fearful of the unknown. After registering at reception, I took a seat in the waiting room and before long, Katy the nurse assigned to me called me into the Chemo Suite. She escorted me to her area and offered me the choice of a bed or a reclining chair. I chose the chair and while Katy was getting things ready I went to the bathroom to relieve myself. Katy then went over the entire procedure, orientated me to the surroundings, equipment and in general to what I should expect during my treatments. She gave me print outs about the drugs I was getting and reassured me that I should not experience any vomiting, but if for some reason I should vomit, I was to report it and the doctor would order something to avoid this happening again. She also informed me of certain side effects to be aware of and should they occur, I needed to report them promptly to the doctor.

I was so happy that Randy and Brad were with me for this first session. Their support was important to me but also their presence was a distraction from all the fears going through me during this time.

The day progressed without event and it was time to disconnect the IV so that I could go home. I thanked Katy for her compassion in helping me get through this first difficult day. Her approach made all the difference in allaying the anxiety and fears that had consumed me earlier in the day. Randy, Brad and I left the hospital to make the forty-five minute journey home. During the drive home, I felt some abdominal cramping and was relieved that I made it home before the loose stools took effect.

* * * * *

Most of my chemo sessions went about the same, with the same side effects. I experienced, nausea, chest tightness, gastro intestinal disturbances, visual disturbances, fatigue, dizziness, headache, flushing of face and upper chest, usually around day three after chemo, restlessness, and sore throat and in the latter treatments neuropathy in my fingers and toes. The steroids caused me to be restless, almost bouncing off the walls, kept me awake at night and increased my appetite beyond belief...I ate more than most large men and very often. It seemed like I was hungry every three hours and had to feed that hunger.

After my second chemo session I developed severe heartburn. Dr. M.O. ordered meds for this. Also around the fifth day following chemo, I developed a severe sore throat...I could hardly swallow. The doctor ordered medication for this as well that I would swish around my mouth, and then swallow It helped to get rid of the sore throat in a faster period of time.

* * * * *

In April 2011, Kevin came from northern Alberta for a visit...I hadn't seen him in six months. I tried to get Kev to go to chemo with me, so he could see what it was all about, but chemo had to be delayed, as my white blood count was too low. The doctor ordered Neupogen for me to help build up my white blood count in between chemo sessions. I had to give myself one injection per day as ordered...sometimes six days straight or other times for four or five days consecutively. I enjoyed my visit with Kev but wished that he could have shared the chemo experience with me.

In early May I bought myself a wig, dark brown with highlights and a good shorter length for me. On May 8th, Mother's Day Randy shaved my head as I had been pulling out hair for the past couple of weeks and my head was becoming patches of hair. After the hair was all gone from my head, I discovered that I had a nicely shaped head. I know this was more upsetting for Randy as I saw tears in his eyes after he finished shaving my head. I felt sad but also realized that having no hair was the least of my worries.

The day before Mother's Day, I received the most beautiful bouquet of fresh flowers from Kev and Brad. They never forgot me and always managed to make me cry...oh how I miss them both!

In May one of the doctor's at the hospital related to me that the cancer I now had was probably as a result of all the radiation I had twenty-five years earlier. The radiation cured me then but brought the cancer back this time, with a vengeance. This information was not only interesting but also understandable...

I also saw my Ophthalmologists in May for a visual field test as well as a measurement of my eye pressure. The pressure in my right eye was 27, which is way too high. The doctor likes to see the pressure settle around 16. As a result he started me on eye drops for glaucoma, but when I saw the doctor about a month later the pressure in my eye was just as high, so he changed the eye drops to a different prescription. I had to return to see him again in six weeks time. At that time the pressure had come down significantly, so I was to remain on these eye drops and follow up again with the doctor in six months. The doctor felt strongly that the elevated pressure in my eyes was a direct result of the steroids I was receiving.

Chemo became more difficult with each treatment. My energy level got zapped and I was so fatigued all of the time. I would fall asleep on the couch for a couple of hours in the afternoon, and then again in the early evening. Then I would go to bed for the night and sleep again. I tried to counteract the fatigue by going outside each day for some fresh air. I would walk to the end of my driveway, which is quite long, and then walk back again. This was all the strength and energy I could muster in one day. The only other energy rush I had was in preparing supper each day. This in itself was quite a production. I often would get my vegetables ready in cold water in the early afternoon, then rest before having to finish the rest of the meal in the evening.

* * * * *

I had problems with my PICC line several times when there wasn't any blood return. The nurses did everything in their power to encourage the PICC line to work but often to no avail. The nurses as a last resort would have to speak to the doctor to get and order for a chest x-ray as well as "cath flo". The chest x-ray would be done immediately to verify whether or not the PICC line catheter was indeed correctly positioned. If the x-ray was okay then the nurse would inject "cath flo" into my PICC line, it works like draino to remove any blockages or blood clots in the line. After injecting this the nurse would label the line and the following day the line would have to be aspirated before use. Usually, the line worked well after this procedure.

Every Wednesday since having the PICC line inserted, I had an RN from Home Care come to my house to flush my PICC line and change the dressing. In June the doctor ordered four days of hydration for me following chemo sessions, because I couldn't drink enough fluids to properly hydrate myself. Now for four days following chemo an RN would come to the house, hook me up to an IV for four hours, then they would return to discontinue the IV and heparinize the PICC line.

* * * * *

On June 11, 2011, I had an interim CT scan. The results of this were good. It showed that the chemo was effective in reducing the large tumour above my left kidney by two-thirds. Other lymph nodes were reduced to half their size. I guess the treatments were worth all the horrible stuff I was going through.

On July 26, 2011, I had chemo and also had to have a blood transfusion of two units of blood. My haemoglobin was only 86; the normal range is 120 - 140. I had been very short of breath prior to the transfusion and was extremely weak. I couldn't walk from one room to another without gasping for air. A couple of days following the transfusion I started to feel stronger and at least I was not labouring to get my breath.

In August 2011, Kevin came to visit from Ft. McMurray, Alberta. Kevin was hopeful that this time around he might be able to attend a chemo session with me; however, both weeks that he was home my blood results were too low for chemo to take place. It was very unfortunate because Brad had attended several chemo sessions with me in his frequent visits home this year. Oh well, at least I wasn't feeling really sick while Kev was visiting, so I could enjoy my time with him a little better.

In just over six months from starting chemotherapy, my chemo sessions were postponed seven or eight times. This was very difficult for me because it made chemo drag on for much longer than I had anticipated.

Finally on October 4, 2011, I had my last chemo treatment, # 12 and also another blood transfusion, this time with one unit of blood. What a thrill this was to have completed chemo. I went up to the front of the chemo suite and rang the victory bell. How happy this made Randy and me also, but it would have been more exciting if there were more nurses and patients there to witness this great feat. Due to the late hour that my chemo and transfusion were finished, most of the patients and nurses had left, there were only a handful left to share in my joy and as luck would have it, the nurses remaining were a few of my favourites...how special!

On October 11, 2011, I had another CT scan done...this one was done as a result of chemo being finished. The doctor will give me the results on October 17th.

* * * * *

When I was to start chemotherapy, I had great fears. Mostly, my fears were of being sick, vomiting all the time and losing a tremendous amount of weight.

H. Anne Sinotte

I didn't want to look like a cancer victim, nor did I want to be pitied. My oncology team assured me that I would be put on a stringent regime of anti-nausea medications. They informed me that if I vomited once, that would be once too many, and medications would be reviewed and adjusted accordingly. I was told that I would be given a couple of the strongest, most potent chemo drugs available, so I wasn't convinced that I wouldn't suffer with nausea as a side effect.

An important thing to remember about chemotherapy is that every person will have a different experience. In the first place there are so many different chemo drugs. Some drugs work better on certain cancers. A doctor will order the drug most suitable for each client, taking into account, the patient's general health, weight, type of cancer, extent of cancer, including metastases and what the patient might be able to tolerate.

My experience with chemotherapy seemed so unique compared to many of the stories I previously heard. I gained twenty pounds during my therapy and had the healthiest appetite. I couldn't get enough to eat. When I finished one meal I was planning the next one. It got to the point that when Randy and I were together, he would guard his plate

H. Anne Sinotte

for fear that I would eat his food when mine was all gone.

I attributed this appetite enhancement and weight gain to the steroids I was taking to prevent nausea. The steroids were definitely effective in controlling the nausea, but in order to have that, I had to put up with other side effects of the drug such as: increased appetite, weight gain, hyperactivity and difficulty sleeping.

The hyperactivity and difficulty sleeping were especially bothersome. I would often be up at 3:00 in the morning, after tossing and turning for an hour or so prior. Many times I would venture into the kitchen at that time and make homemade soup or prepare a meal to put in the freezer for another day. Because of the early hour in which I arose, I would find myself napping several times a day. Of course some of this was general fatigue caused by the chemo.

Fatigue was the most crippling side effect I had to deal with. I probably slept on average anywhere from 12 - 16 hours per day. I tried going outdoors for fresh air, doing mild exercises, cooking or carrying out light housekeeping chores to avoid sleeping but it was to no avail. Sleep overpowered

H. Anne Sinotte

everything else; it was like a beacon pulling me into its range. It was like a broken record when phone calls came in, Randy would tell the caller "Annie is sleeping, resting or lying down." Anything I did, any activity at all, reduced me to sheer weakness and fatigue. An hour in the grocery store felt like eight hours of shopping. Towards the end I would be literally hanging off the grocery cart, with a heaviness filling my eyes. If I planned an outing, I would have to have a nap before I ventured out. After my first couple of treatments I had an epiphany. I realized that chemotherapy and this cancer had become my full time job. It was senseless trying to fight something that I could not change. I needed to forget about everything else in my life and take my treatments, live with the side effects and welcome whatever rest my body required. Chemo zaps the body of all energy and strength; therefore, my job was to nurture my body through rest, exercise, fresh air, nourishment and sleep. This new way of thinking focused on the positive...self restoration!

My chemo sessions were very long in duration. The minimum time spent in the chemo suite was five hours. Most people averaged two to three hours of treatment time. During this time I tried to keep busy by reading, knitting or writing. Sometimes I

H. Anne Sinotte

would doze off for a short period of time, but I generally tried not to sleep, because I have been told that I snore very loudly. Treatment days were long and I often felt sorry for Randy, Brad or whoever accompanied me to my appointments. The reclining chairs or the beds in the chemo suite were most comfortable. There was a TV and telephone for each patient's use and even the Internet was available.

One thing I learned during chemo was to include family members and friends in the process. Invite them to accompany you on lab or doctor's day or to take you and sit with you through chemotherapy. This gives them a sense of involvement and sharing in the ordeal, as well as learning more about the process. The more people are included the more understanding they will be, and the more educated about this horrible disease.

Because of the length of time I spent in the chemo suite and the frequency of my treatments, I became quite close to most of the RN's. They were so wonderful to Randy and me and really to any of my guests. They were all so passionate about what they did and treated the patients with the utmost courtesy and dignity. These nurses truly cared about their clients. If I were concerned about something, they

H. Anne Sinotte

would help me come up with a possible solution. If I needed to cry, they would give me a shoulder to cry on. If I needed support, they would hold my hand and if I needed to vent, they would listen. The nurses and the chemo suite became a "safe haven" for me. I felt strong feelings of security when I was there; so much so that I dealt with a form of withdrawal once my chemo treatments were over.

H. Anne Sinotte

*Hope sees the invisible, feels the intangible, and
achieves the impossible.*
- Author Unknown

Chapter Twenty-Four
Living With a Terminal Illness

October 17, 2011, I think of today as D-Day. My appointment at the hospital with Dr. M.O. was at 2:15 pm. This was a long day of worry and anxiety because I would be getting the results of the CAT scan done a week ago, the first CAT scan done since completing my chemotherapy. I had all the necessary blood work done and the results remained quite low. It will take time for my levels to return to normal once again, after all the destruction the chemo had done to my body.

It was finally time to see the doctor. He gave me a copy of my CAT scan but also told me he was pleased with the results. The tumours and lymph nodes continue to shrink, so the chemo was definitely effective. When I asked him for a prognosis he related that at best I had a twenty percent chance of living two years. The average outcome for a Stage four lung cancer was nine to twelve months. I know that I wasn't prepared to hear the words that were now echoing through my brain. The doctor advised me to do whatever I needed or wanted to do while the quality of life I was experiencing lasted. At that time he would not give me clearance to go to Florida in January 2012, as he wanted me to have another CT scan at that time, before a decision would be made. He did suggest that I go to Florida until the end of December, but that was not feasible for us with the plans we had already made for the upcoming holiday season.

This was not the news either Randy or I had hoped for, it left me numb to the point that I couldn't ask any further questions. It was like the wind was knocked out of my sails. How could the chemo have been so effective, yet my time be so short? This didn't make sense to me. All the agony and horrors of chemo to possibly only get two more years. I was devastated...so much to do and so little time. I cried all the way home from the hospital, which didn't help Randy because he was also very upset.

So many thoughts were raging through my head. How does one prepare for death? What will it be like? Will I suffer with breathing problems or pain? Will I be able to do my own care or will someone

H. Anne Sinotte

have to wash and toilet me? Will I lose the use of my legs and become bedridden? Will I be able to stay at home or will my days end in the hospital? How will Randy, Kevin and Brad cope with losing me? I think of all the future times I will miss...times with Randy and the boys. My heart is already breaking!

The worst part of this was having to break the news to the boys. It was so difficult telling Kevin and Brad that their mom was dying. October 17th was not just the day I received this bad news, it was also Brad's birthday, so I chose not to tell him the news until the following day and I telephoned Kevin that same evening to tell him. I knew that they were both quite upset and would have to absorb this information and come to grips with it in their own way. Life sure is not fair!!!!

I held off telling everyone else until Kev and Brad knew. I have no secrets, it is what it is and I can't change anything. I will continue to fight this demon for as long as I can. I have had a positive attitude from the onset and I won't let this cancer get the best of me...NOT YET!

*****

H. Anne Sinotte

Trying to maintain a positive attitude after being told your cancer is incurable, therefore, rendering your life as terminal is extremely difficult. There isn't a fleeting moment that this predicament leaves one's mind. There are so many questions, concerns yet unanswered, but dwelling on this negativity would only make matters worse.

Once I had put my health status out in the open by telling my sons, family and friends, I was able to move on. At first I took a couple of days to have a "pity" party for which I was the guest of honour. I blurted out my thoughts, feelings, and fears to anyone who would listen, much like one would blow a horn at a New Year's Eve party. I needed to vent, to hear the words being said out loud in order to know that what was happening was indeed real.

My family was in turmoil over this news, so it was time to hide my weakness away and let my strength shine through. I only knew of one way to do this and that was to LIVE life as fully and as joyous as possible. There were going to be no second chances or promised tomorrows. I must live in the here and now.

I decided that I would not allow negativity to poison my days; therefore, I would avoid any one who

H. Anne Sinotte

chose this unproductive behaviour. I was going to make my days as happy and productive as possible.

* * * * *

Towards the end of November, the first of our Christmas plans unfolded or so I thought. Randy and I headed to Whitby to my Brother Mark's house for our sibling Christmas with my family. We walked in the door and the "Surprise, Happy 60th" hit me like a ton of bricks. Shock came over me as I had not expected or wanted anything special done for my birthday, which was still a week and a half away. Apparently, my brothers insisted that this birthday was special and should be marked by having a party.

Once the initial shock subsided, I was able to greet all of my guests. I'm glad my brothers had the good sense to keep things simple. The guests were all members of my family, with the exception of my friends, Pat and Tom and Lynn and Paul.

As the evening progressed, I started to relax and enjoyed the time I spent with everyone. Care was taken in planning this event. All of my favourite foods were served; cabbage rolls, perogies, shish-ka-bobs, ham, scalloped potatoes, stuffed pasta shells, Caesar salad...I couldn't have asked for anything better. My favourite music was played, the birthday cake was delicious, as were all the foods in the main course. I received lovely gifts, but the greatest gift was the memories I was left with at the end of the evening.

I thanked my brothers and their wives for all the thought and energy they put in to this evening...it was a delightful surprise.

* * * * *

A week later Carolyn my neighbour across the street, held another surprise birthday party for me under the pretence that this was a Christmas Open House. Many of the neighbours from our community were present. Once again this was a lovely afternoon mingling with everyone. Carolyn did a great job making this a special day for me. I was so impressed that she thought enough of me to create this special time and memory for me.

I remember commenting after this second party that the cancer wasn't going to kill me; all the surprise parties might instead.

It was still two days until my birthday. On the

actual day of my birthday, December 6th, Randy and I spent the day shopping then went out for a delicious dinner afterward...it was another enjoyable day.

Now with all the birthday celebrations out of the way, I could concentrate on Christmas.

*****

Christmas was approaching so what a wonderful opportunity to rejoice and celebrate life's mysteries. I was looking forward to Kevin and Brad coming home from Alberta to celebrate the season. This would be the first Christmas together in about four years so definitely something to look forward to.

Preparations were in full swing. I had the inside of the house all decorated including the Christmas tree up and decorated by mid-November. I so love the lights and colours of Christmas, the carols, and the food...it has always been my favourite time of year. Every day I put Christmas music on to listen to and at night I tried to find Christmas programs to watch on television.

I did Christmas baking keeping in mind the favourites of Randy and the boys. I planned a

Christmas Day menu and shopped accordingly. I did my Christmas shopping bit by bit, depending on how I felt and of course when the weather permitted. Some shopping I did over the phone through the catalogue. I accepted invitations to friends and family homes, to the church for choir performances and also invited folks into my home.

Then the boys arrived home, first Brad on December 22nd, then Kevin on December 28th. We were celebrating Christmas later on December 28th and 29th due to Kevin's work schedule. It was so great being altogether, laughing, crying, debating, talking and watching television.

The day that Kevin arrived, he and Brad presented me with my belated birthday gift. They had me close my eyes and once positioned, then told me to open my eyes. There folded before me was a beautiful quilt in my favourite colours of red and green, inscribed in one of the squares was the "Footprints" prayer. Next Kevin and Brad said that they would open the quilt and hold it up so that I could see the size of it. The quilt was huge, but that is not what caught my eyes. The quilt told a story...there was photos silk-screened onto the quilt of the boys from infants to present day. There were twelve photos in total, including a couple with our

H. Anne Sinotte

wonderful dog Gypsy, who is no longer with us, and a couple photos of my mom and dad, who also have left this world.

As I looked at this incredible gift, I cried, so many memories re-created on this magnificent, soon to be heirloom. Brad commented that even if I had to go into the hospital, the quilt could go with me so that I always would have my family with me. Again I cried.

I was amazed at how thoughtful this gift was coming from my two sons. Boys don't usually have such personal, sentimental ideas. I was totally blown away by this and still feel the same way. Other than the gift of my two wonderful sons, this by far has to be the greatest gift I've ever received. I am so proud and blessed to have Kevin and Brad in my life.

* * * * *

It was a wonderful Christmas, somewhat bittersweet, but wonderful just the same.

We had a special family outing on December 30th. For Christmas Randy bought me four tickets to "The Wizard of Oz" stage presentation in Toronto, so we attended this as a family. Afterwards, Brad took us all out for dinner as his Christmas gift to each of us. What an enjoyable, memorable day for me, a real delight.

As all good things must come to an end, the boys flew back to Alberta, Brad on New Year's Day and Kevin on January 3, 2012. I'm so thankful for this time we had together...it was very special.

In essence I lived Christmas of 2011 as if it were my last. To some that may sound like negative thinking, but in actuality it is quite positive. I enjoyed everything about the festive season to the hilt, to the best of my capabilities. I spent each waking moment breathing the joys and delights of the wonders of Christmas. I don't believe that many people can say this. If I am privileged to be alive for Christmas of 2012, I will once again embrace this glorious season.

In reality, I guess my mind set is to live every day as if it were my last. I thank God for every day of life and try to show my gratitude through my actions. It's not that I do super exciting things each day; instead I do what makes me happy. That could mean visiting with a friend, cooking a special meal, having a nap, having a telephone conversation with

H. Anne Sinotte

my kids, knitting, writing, the list goes on and on...I do what I want to do within my physical limitations. For some this may be boring...skydiving may better meet their needs, and that is also okay. Each individual must follow his or her heart and do what is right for them.

Some days I am content doing nothing other than thinking, viewing old photos and recalling memorable events. There is a comfort achieved in doing just this. Also memories can sustain us and give us drive and hope. I never want to lose sight of hope because that would influence my existence.

There are no longer any second chances promised. Each day is the here and now. Live it, embrace it and above all have no regrets.

*****

The challenges faced with this type of prognosis are surreal. It is sometimes difficult to know what to say or what actions to take with certain individuals. There are people that I don't see on a regular basis. What is the appropriate action to take? Do I say goodbye to them and thank them for being a part of my life? Is that morbid thinking? As much as I might hope to beat the odds, what if I am not faced with this opportunity again?

I have found that when I'm leaving that person's company, I might hug them slightly longer than I did before, or I might let my eyes linger on their eyes for a longer period of time in hopes that the person understands my hesitation.

As time goes by, I am aware of a change in my demeanour, my responses can be abrupt and verging on rude. At this time I am not aware that the cancer has spread to my brain. Am I using this as a defence mechanism to distance myself from others? I have also been very touchy regarding certain subjects. I am not very empathetic to people who cry "whoa for me", all the time and expect the world to cater to their every whim. Often these are people who do nothing to help themselves and take advantage of other people's kind gestures. I guess this is my bitter side, because with all the health issues I've had to deal with, I've never once asked anyone for help...people have offered their services to me for whatever my need was at the time. Does this thinking make me wrong or am I just a fool?

I have noticed that when I go shopping I don't want to spend money on myself, especially when it comes to clothing. The realism kicks in.why do I

H. Anne Sinotte

need more clothes when I'm going to die soon? I will put clothing back on the shelf, or rack without giving it another thought.

Each day as soon as my eyes open, my thoughts go immediately to my cancer and the death sentence I've been given. It is so hard to shake these feelings and put them out of my mind. It is all consuming. I try my best to get through the days not showing these feelings to others. It is unimaginable for someone who is not going through something like this.

The comment I've heard the most that bothers me the most is, "anyone of us could step off a curb tomorrow and be hit and killed by a passing vehicle." This comment is made I realize in hopes of showing how delicate life can be. However, I do not find much consolation in hearing this anymore and often respond with, "of course I'm also included in this potential type of demise, but have the added knowledge of having a terminal illness, so it is not really an equal equation."

I also find myself being cut off from the rest of the world. At a time when I need people the most, they are backing away from me. Why is this so? Is it because they do not know what to say to me or how

H. Anne Sinotte

to act in my presence? Is it the fact that it is difficult just being around a dying person, it's not fun or exciting...in fact it can be downright depressing. Whatever the answer may be it has left me with feelings of alienation and feeling unwanted.

I have tried to remain positive throughout this ordeal, but I've seen some of that positive attitude diminish. It isn't easy to be positive when those around you ignore you. A lot of days I feel truly alone, as if I am going through this by myself. Because I feel this way I've decided that any decisions to be made from here on in, I will make by myself without consulting anyone else. It may seem rather selfish, but maybe it is time I became more selfish, regarding my questionable future.

Sometimes I wonder what it will be like as my condition deteriorates. Will I be flooded then with curious onlookers, coming around under the pretence of helping me because they "care" so much about me? I don't want or need that kind of pity.

I know that I am writing this section on one of my more depressing days. In general the support I've received has been awesome; it is just recently that the ties have broken. Perhaps people feel that

H. Anne Sinotte

because I generally look good, I can't be as sick as I am. Also for the most part people lead busy lives and don't necessarily want to surround themselves with illness and a dying person.

*****

One major accomplishment I achieved with Randy's assistance was making funeral arrangements. We consulted with our sons as to what their expectations were at the time of our demise, and then we pooled their thoughts and our wishes together to form a plan. We have simplified our arrangements to cremation, followed by a Memorial Celebration of Life, at an appropriate time afterwards. Our ashes will be buried at the feet of one of my parent's graves and there will be a ground marker with our names and dates. I have all the funeral arrangements noted in a special book given to me by a representative from the funeral home. By pre-arranging this will make this a less daunting task for survivors, when the time comes.

Going through the process of making funeral arrangements was to say the least, draining. This is the final aspect of one's existence; it requires careful thought and rational thought. There were many times that tears fell uncontrollably from my

H. Anne Sinotte

eyes. I couldn't fight the finality of my life coming to an end but I would continue to trudge forward with the arrangements because I knew this had to be done before my health status deteriorated.

I did not want my family at the time of my death to be at the mercy of the funeral home. This is usually a very emotional time for family members and they don't need the added burden of people capitalizing on their emotions. By pre-arranging everything, I can orchestrate final arrangements to be carried out in accordance with my wishes.

*****

Everyone has heard of the term "bucket" list. I think having a bucket list is a wonderful, sensible idea. Each person will have different things on their list. Some will have a lengthy list while others a fairly short list, it all depends on the prognosis, but more importantly one's health status.

I am no different than anyone else. I made a bucket list and it is not very long. My list consists of the following but it is not necessarily written in order of importance to me:
1. Make funeral arrangements.
2. Visit Graceland in Memphis, Tennessee, USA.

H. Anne Sinotte

3. Visit the World of Golf, St. Augustine, Florida, USA.
4. Be healthy enough to see, hold & welcome my first grandchild, due May 25/12
5. Finish writing my book -- Challenges and Blessings.
6. Get my book published.
7. Write journals to Kevin and Brad.
8. Make lists of which personal belongings I will leave to whom.
9. Read the Bible from cover to cover -- Old & New Testaments.
10. Have Randy buy a collector car or a "fun" car.
11. To be able to say a proper goodbye to family and friends.

I am not doing too badly with realizing my choices on this list. I have made funeral arrangements, I hope to visit Graceland in April on our trip home from Florida, I have visited the World of Golf...I wanted Randy and myself to enjoy this together and we did along with our friends Fuzz and Marilyn...it was a great day! Awaiting the birth of my first grandchild is my biggest goal at present. I am almost finished writing my book and I now have some insight regarding getting the book published. I am still working on the journals to Kev and Brad, as well as the lists regarding my personal

H. Anne Sinotte

belongings. I am almost finished reading the Bible, even though I still don't understand much of what is written in the Bible. Randy has bought a 2003 Corvette convertible as his fun car. It is the Corvette he wanted, the 50th anniversary edition. My goodbyes to family and friends will come at the appropriate time.

In the next month, I should be able to complete four of the items on my bucket list. When those items are complete, I will only have four outstanding items. Hopefully, by the autumn of 2012 most of my list will be achieved but if it doesn't happen, at least I know I took a huge stab at it.

* * * * *

Today is March 11, 2012, and I had my first hysterical outburst since being diagnosed with my present cancer. The past couple of weeks I have been drawing into myself more and more, having a difficult time getting through the days. I listen to people's conversations, hear their joy about different things, listen to them making plans for the future, the fun they had here or what they did there. Although I'm happy for them in the lives they are living, I'm also resentful of the life I've been dealt, unable to make long-term plans, being too tired to

H. Anne Sinotte

have fun or to short of breath to take part in various activities. These feelings have been building up in me for months now. Randy had just come in from golfing and I once again spent the day all by myself. I tried to explain to him what I was thinking and feeling but I don't think he got it...how could he? he isn't the one dying! I started crying hysterically and shouting as well. "Why won't anyone just listen to me, let me talk about what this is doing to me, what my fears are? I feel so alone as if I'm going through this by myself. No one wants to be with a sick person and no one wants to listen to my dilemma." These are all concerns I through out to Randy, but he still wasn't getting it. He admitted that he is in denial, that he doesn't want me to die, he can't accept that and he doesn't want to be alone for the rest of his life. Then he crashed the coffee table to the floor, letting loose pent up anger and fear. On that ended any hopes of discussing these problems any further.

After this incident, I realized my need to pursue discussions on this matter. Therefore, I made a decision that upon return to Canada, I would seek out professional psychological help at the oncology clinic I attend. I believe that Randy would also benefit from counselling but he must come to that realization himself.

H. Anne Sinotte

* * * * *

In October 2011, shortly after I received my prognosis, Kevin shared some special news with Randy and me. He informed us that he and his girlfriend Nathalie were expecting a baby. My initial reaction may not have been as joyous as it should have been. Disturbing thoughts went through my mind, "Will I be alive when the baby is born? Will I get to see and hold the baby? Will I get to enjoy any of the usual grandparent things?" It all seemed so bittersweet. There is nothing in the world I wanted more than to be a grandma, now it is going to happen on the heels of my terminal illness.

As we all needed time to absorb my prognosis, now I needed time to absorb this news. When the concept of this baby started to sink in and become a reality, I tried to set aside what was happening to me. This wasn't about me, it was about Kevin and Nathalie and their future. Other questions surfaced such as; are they going to raise this child together? Will they live together? Where will they live? How can they afford this baby? These were all questions I would later address with Kevin. He was honest with his answers, in that he didn't have the answers. All he could honestly say is that he and

Nathalie were trying to work things out. I realized that I had to back off and give them their space. These were decisions only the two of them could make. In the meantime, Kevin asked me not to tell anyone else about this pregnancy. They wanted to safely make it through the first trimester before sharing this pregnancy with the rest of the world. A wise decision I thought on their part. All I wanted was the best possible outcome for my grandchild.

As the months slipped away I was in tuned to the changes going on in Kevin's life. I picked up on subtle changes, like the way he included Nathalie in most conversations about his future, the fact that they were spending more time together, and the two of them were together for all baby developments like the first ultrasound, the 3D ultrasound and shopping for the baby.

They discovered at the first ultrasound that Nathalie was carrying a boy. This pleased both of them because they were hoping for a boy. When I viewed the video of the ultrasound, I cried it was so awesome. This made it all so real now. This precious little bundle was coming into our lives.

March 2012 rolled around and Kevin consulted us on buying a house. This house would be shared by

Nathalie, the baby and Kevin. What good news this was to hear his plans. Maybe at 33 years of age he is finally starting to mature. He was adamant about making a proper home for Nathalie and the baby.

We guided Kev the best we could in regards to real estate, mortgages and taxes. Kevin purchased a beautiful 2300 square foot, three-bedroom home, which could easily be converted into a four bedroom if the need presented itself. I am so proud that Kevin is manning up to his responsibilities…in my heart of hearts, I know that he will make a good dad; he has always loved children and has a good rapport with them.

Now with wintering in Florida, the only shopping I do is baby shopping. I have bought so many cute outfits for this little one, as well as some other baby items. This expected grandbaby has given me reason to fight this disease with every fibre of my being. I must live to see and hold this precious gift.

*****

One of my fears is that of being forgotten after my death. When I spoke about making funeral arrangements earlier in this chapter, Randy and I consulted our sons about what to do with our ashes

H. Anne Sinotte

after cremation. One son suggested spreading the ashes in places that held meaning for each of us, such as the golf course for Randy. Our other son stated that he would prefer some sort of marker or monument with our names inscribed, to show that we once walked on this earth. A place that he or anyone else could go, to see our names and pay respect.

My thinking was much the same; I didn't want my ashes to blow away in the wind never to be seen again. This was too cold and final for me. I also wanted my name on a marker in a cemetery for anyone interested to be able to view, possibly even for future generations to visit.

I would like to think that I made some connection or impact with those I leave behind, that the person I am and everything that I stand for will not be lost or forgotten upon death.

Sometimes I am amazed at how some people connect spiritually with others and at the most meaningful times. At the time of writing this chapter, American friends, Fuzz and Marilyn, who winter in our Florida community, presented me with a gift a couple of days before they were heading back north. The gift was a Willow Tree (trademark)

Figurine entitled Forget-me-not. This figurine is a thinking of you piece represented with the message, "timeless friendship and love that spans any distance." A female holding a bouquet of forget-me-not flowers portrays the figurine itself. Unfortunately, my initial reaction upon opening this gift was not a true display of the sentiment I later felt in my heart. The thoughtfulness of the gift givers and the accompanying sentiment, *forget-me-not*, helped to negate the fears I had of being forgotten. I know whenever I look at this figurine; I will feel the friendship and love shown to me by Fuzz and Marilyn and be grateful that they were a part of my life, a life not to be forgotten.

* * * * *

The most recurring thought that weighs heavily on my heart is leaving the people I love, brothers, sister-in-laws, mother and father-in-laws, nieces, nephews, aunts, uncles, good friends and especially Randy, Kevin and Brad. I recall a comment I made in the past, that a life well lived, giving and showing love to those nearest and dearest to one requires no special or final goodbye. I guess that I felt that the people left behind would always know that they were loved so in death it wasn't necessary for them to hear the words "I love you." I still partly agree

H. Anne Sinotte

with my past rationale, except now that I am on the precipice of life my feelings and thoughts go deeper. My previous thinking seems understated.

How do I say goodbye? Will I know when the time will be right or will things happen so quickly that I won't be able to say these last words to the people I care about? Provocative thoughts but the feelings linked with these thoughts are even more astounding. Some people might wonder why any of this is even an issue, just live life to the fullest and deal with the end when it comes. I wish that I could be so casual about such finality, but that is impossible, I am too sentimental for that type of thinking.

I am not a fool in the sense that I think I can script my demise, instead I would prefer to think of this as closure for myself and the people I care most about. A final tribute to the relationships we shared, relationships that contributed to defining who I was as a person.

*****

Feelings of grief consume me over leaving my husband and sons. I worry about a multitude of things concerning each of them.

H. Anne Sinotte

Randy has been my best friend throughout the thirty-seven years of our marriage. We have always made major decisions together and often minor decisions as well. We have been sounding boards for each other. Together, we have provided guidance for our sons, all their lives. We started our lives together with a good foundation but we were not heavily weighted with material possessions. In our years together we built on that foundation a strong and loving home, through hard work and sacrifice.

Both Randy and I are very much homebodies…we are far from being social butterflies or party animals, home and family always came first. We enjoy our sedate lifestyle. I'm worried that once I'm gone, Randy will lose this security that was so important to both of us.

Randy does not come from a closely-knit family. His father is deceased; his mother lives a distance away, as does his sister, and his two brothers have been estranged from him in recent years. This leaves my family…my parents are deceased, two of my brothers are in fairly new second marriages, so they just aren't in the same place of life that Randy is. My youngest brother Mark, his wife and family

H. Anne Sinotte

are probably the closest to Randy and I believe they will remain in contact with him. As for our friends, I don't know what will happen, as they were mostly my friends and Randy adopted them. I know he will not push himself on anyone because he doesn't want to be a fifth wheel. Perhaps Randy will relocate to Alberta where our sons reside. This may be one of the most comfortable solutions and the least lonely for him.

My concerns for Kev and Brad are different. They are both self-sufficient because they have both lived on their own for several years now. As the matriarch of the family, I kept certain customs and traditions alive and I believe to maintain some level of stability in life these traditions are necessary and need to be continued. Getting together at Easter, Thanksgiving, Christmas and birthdays are so important to keep family ties from being severed. Will this happen. I don't know, I can only hope and pray that it does.

I am saddened to think of not being around for all these special occasions, watching my boys grow older and mature, not being there for career changes or developments, possible marriages, or just seeing each of them happy and settled with a significant other. There are so many little things that warm a

H. Anne Sinotte

mother's heart, like being there to offer guidance, or an opinion on different issues, hearing that mom makes the best potato salad, lasagne or other foods, having one of the boys phone for a certain recipe, or receiving a hug from these young men who tower over me, knowing the hug serves their benefit as much as my own. These are the things that tug at my heart. These are the things that will make it so difficult to leave this world.

The fact that I am going to be a first time grandma is delightfully sad. There is nothing in this world that I wanted more than a grand baby. Although I am thrilled that this is happening, I am also saddened at the thought that I will not be able to watch him grow up and share the wonders of life with him. I guess I will have to be grateful for every minute I am able to spend with him and I will give him all the love that is in my heart, in the same manner that I give that love to Randy, Kevin and Brad. This love will have to last them forever, just as my heart will be filled with the love they have given me, which I will take with me for all eternity.

H. Anne Sinotte

A bend in the road is not the end of the road----unless you fail to make the turn.
- *Author Unknown*

Chapter Twenty-Five
Epilogue

The sun still rises every morning and sets every evening...life goes on. With every dawning there is the promise of renewal and hope. I thank the Lord for every day of life and for walking along side of me not just in the troubling times but also in the good times. I don't know how I would have gotten through the many challenges in my life without a strong faith. I believe that there is more and better than what we have in this life on earth. I know that I am one of God's children and He will lovingly embrace me and take me to a paradise, where I will no longer suffer any of the hardships I did in my present life. My faith will bring me to that place.

I will carry on living my life to the best of my abilities. I will take one day at a time and welcome the good days as opportunities for renewed strength, to counteract whatever bad days come my way. I will always try to have something to look forward to in order to keep a positive attitude and to encourage hope to flourish. I will never lose sight of the endless possibilities that can occur, when one believes.

I have surmised that there is no way to prepare for one's death. It just happens; it will unfold in whatever way it is meant to...it is out of our control.

I thank my husband Randy for his loyalty and devotion throughout our married life. He has always supported me through every challenge; he has been my "rock." This latest and most difficult challenge, my terminal cancer has been devastating for our entire family, but Randy has remained strong and true. He has helped me through so many aspects of this disease that many, many people would not have been able to cope with. As I've said before Randy is my strongest weakness and I love him for all that he is.

I thank Kevin and Brad for the love and support they have given me all their lives. They protected me and always made me feel special. They have endured so many tragedies with me, more than children should have to at such young ages. I believe that even though they are hurting deep in their hearts, all of this has made them stronger young men. I love them beyond any words.

H. Anne Sinotte

I am grateful to my family and friends for their love, support and understanding. Each one has helped to make my journey less daunting. I love each and every one of you.

I would be remiss not to mention the wonderful doctors, nurses and caregivers who entered my life according to each need and to the ones who are still significant in the journey yet to come. I have been blessed with professional excellence and I offer my heartfelt gratitude to each of you for the role you played in my life.

* * * * *

Writing this book has been an accomplishment that I am very proud of. I was encouraged by my psychologist over five years ago to write this book. It has taken me at least four years to complete. Finishing this book was my goal, having the book published is my dream, so I will continue to dream until the dream becomes real.

I am extremely grateful to my psychologist for suggesting I write about my experiences and I am perplexed at his faith in my writing skills. Writing this book has proven to be a therapeutic exercise for me. It has enabled me to put aspects of my accident and illnesses in perspective. It also helped me to address and work through the multitude of emotions running through me, dealing with each one individually. By putting pen to paper, the problems became real and in the case of my present cancer, it initiated elements of the grieving process for me. This book has helped me to find peace.

* * * * *

I cannot predict the future or how my journey will end, but I have learned the following:

I have learned that I have not faced these adversities solely as trials to make me strong. Instead this has been an overwhelming journey that has at times, crippled me, weakened me, disillusioned me, and tested my faith, courage and sense of hope, with the end result that I evolved as an even stronger individual.

Many people with less strength could not have tolerated the events of my journey; therefore, it has been a journey of purpose for me. My purpose was to bear the pain and strife in this life that others could not. I believe that I was "chosen" to a life of **Challenges and Blessings**.

H. Anne Sinotte

H. Anne Sinotte

Made in the USA
Charleston, SC
16 April 2013